O E D I P U S

Of Lucius Annaeus Seneca

OEDIPUS

OF LUCIUS ANNAEUS SENECA

Freely Translated and Adapted
by Michael Elliot Rutenberg

BOLCHAZY-CARDUCCI PUBLISHERS, INC.

for
My Family
🔯

Susan Schulman Literary Agency,
454 W. 44th Street,
New York, NY 10036-5205
212-713-1633/4/5.

Published by
BOLCHAZY-CARDUCCI PUBLISHERS, INC.
1000 Brown Street
Wauconda, Illinois 60084
GENERAL EDITOR: LAURIE K. HAIGHT

Cover: Photo-reproduction of Roman mask of tragedy,
by permission of the Museo Nazionale, Roma.

─────────────

LIBRARY OF CONGRESS CATALOGING-IN-PUBLICATION DATA
Seneca, Lucius Annaeus, ca. 4 B.C.–65 A.D.
    [Oedipus. English]
    Oedipus of Lucius Annaeus Seneca / freely translated and
adapted by Michael Elliot Rutenberg.
        p.   cm.
    ISBN 0-86516-459-2 (pbk. : alk. paper). --
    ISBN 0-86516-463-0 (hardbound : alk. paper).
    1. Oedipus (Greek mythology) Drama. I. Rutenberg, Michael E.
II. Title
PA6666.05R88 1999   99-41314
872'.01--dc21   CIP

iv

TABLE OF CONTENTS

Perhaps it is our destiny to have our mother
the object of our first sexual impulse, and
our father the object of our first murderous
hatred. Our dreams prove this to us....
Today as in the past, many men dream of
sleeping with their mothers....The myth of
Oedipus is our imagination's reaction to these
dreams, and because they produce feelings
of revulsion, so must the legend embody
horrendous self-punishment.

Sigmund Freud (1856–1939)
The Interpretation of Dreams

Rich men, trust not in wealth,
Gold cannot buy you health;
Physic himself must fade,
All things to end are made,
The plague full swift goes by.
I am sick, I must die.
Lord, have mercy on us!

Haste, therefore, each degree,
To welcome destiny.
Heaven is our heritage,
Earth but a player's stage;
Mount we unto the sky.
I am sick, I must die.
Lord, have mercy on us!

Thomas Nashe (1567–1601)
In Plague Time

INTRODUCTION

❂   ❂   ❂

Philosophy, Theatre, and Psychoanalysis

With the recent publication of *Open Minded: Working Out the Logic of the Soul* by Jonathan Lear, the myth of Oedipus continues to challenge each new era, affirming its relevance to those contemporary philosophers, theatre artists, and psychoanalysts willing to reevaluate preconceived notions of behavior. This fascinating book of twelve essays, much of it in defense of Freud's contribution to modern psychology, devotes an entire chapter entitled "Knowingness and Abandonment: An Oedipus for Our Time," to the significance of the Oedipus myth in our own age. Lear maintains that Oedipus understood the Delphic oracle quite well, and that his anxiety-ridden action to avoid its prophecy *is* applicable to our time—not because he is a victim of Freud's famous Oedipus complex, but because Oedipus' rash behavior perfectly reflects our modern need to know that there is an immediate solution to each problem. Lear says "...there is a sickness in this 'knowingness': Reason is being used to jump ahead to a conclusion, as though there is too much anxiety involved in simply asking a question and waiting for the world to answer."

Oedipus, brash in the certainty of his knowledge, and unwilling to accept that he is fallible, rejects Tiresias and accuses him of treachery. Lear brilliantly compares the blind soothsayer to Freud, because both men postulate that we cannot be all-knowing.

Both the material for Lear's insightful essay and the plot for Seneca's almost forgotten work come from Sophocles' (496–406 B.C.) great tragedy *Oedipus Tyrannus*, itself based on ancient mythology familiar to Greek and later Roman audiences.

Mythology

The myth begins with Laius and Jocasta, king and queen of Thebes, who receive a warning from the Delphic oracle that their soon-to-be-born son will kill his father and marry his mother. Immediately after the birth, in an effort to avoid the prophecy, the king and queen have the infant's feet pierced and bound, and have him given to a shepherd who is instructed to abandon the child on the slopes of Mount Cithaeron. The shepherd takes pity on the child and gives it to another shepherd from Corinth, who then brings it to the childless Polybus and Merope, king and queen of Corinth, to be brought up as their own son. They name him Oedipus, which means "swollen foot."

When Oedipus reaches adulthood, he learns from an oracle that he is destined to kill his father and marry his mother. In order to evade his fate, Oedipus leaves Corinth, never to return. During the journey, his chariot and another's meet where three roads cross. Neither occupant is willing to cede the other's right of way. A fight ensues in which hot-headed Oedipus kills the other man—his biological father, King Laius.

Sometime later, Oedipus reaches Thebes and is confronted at the city's gate by the Sphinx, a mythological creature with the head of a woman and the body of a lion. She terrorizes the city by asking all travelers who attempt to pass through the gate a riddle, killing them when they cannot answer it. She asks Oedipus the same cryptic question, but to her surprise, he answers it, causing the outraged Sphinx to leap from her perch and hurl herself against the pointed rocks below to die impaled on their points. Oedipus is then hailed as the city's savior and proclaimed king by the queen's brother, Creon, who is its regent. Oedipus marries Laius' widow—his own mother—and has four children with her: Antigone, Ismene, Eteocles, and Polynices. After ruling benevolently for many years, a plague suddenly descends upon the city.

LUCIUS ANNAEUS SENECA

Lucius Annaeus Seneca, the younger, was born into an affluent family of equestrian rank in Cordova, Spain just before or shortly after the beginning of the Christian era—sometime between 4 B.C. and A.D. 1. His father, Seneca the elder, was a distinguished historian and teacher of rhetoric, famous enough to be cited by Montaigne. The father's oldest son, Annaeus Novatus, was the Roman governor of Southern Greece, and will be remembered as the Roman official before whom the apostle Paul was brought. His youngest son, Mela, was the father of Rome's last great epic poet, Marcus Annaeus Lucanus, whom history recalls as Lucan. As a privileged member of this rich and powerful family, Seneca was brought to Rome as a child and educated in philosophy and rhetoric in preparation for a career in law and politics, which he began in A.D. 31.

The following year in A.D. 32, Seneca held the office of Quaestor (magistrate) and joined the senate. He was so popular and eloquent a senatorial orator that Caligula, in a fit of jealous rage, threatened to have him executed. Seneca took the hint and retired from public life. This may be the period when he began to write his tragedies.

Nine years later in A.D. 41, Caligula was assassinated by his own Praetorian guard, Claudius was declared emperor, and Seneca returned to public life. His comeback occurred at a time of political intrigue, corruption, and assassination—all of which had totally decimated any vestiges of pre-Imperial Rome. Seneca, however, was quickly caught up in the palace power struggles, and at the insistence of Messalina, the Emperor Claudius' second wife, was banished to the desolate and rocky island of Corsica on dubious charges of committing adultery with the Emperor's niece Julia Livilla, sister of the infamous Caligula. Seneca's exile lasted eight difficult years. During this devastating period in his life, he lost his child and first wife, but probably completed the tragedies along with some of his most enduring philosophical essays.

Ironically, by this time, both Roman adaptations of Greek plays as well as indigenous drama, which had been popular in Rome for more than 250 years, were now in decline. Seneca, born at the nadir of this deterioration of high drama, grew to watch its subsequent disappearance as a form of state-sponsored entertainment. Audiences now attended state festivals to see clowns, acrobats, equestrian shows, animal baiting, gladiatorial combats, and chariot races. Ironically, popular taste had changed exactly as he was writing some of Rome's greatest dramas.

The coup de grâce of Roman drama occurred sometime between A.D. 50–53. Two semicircular wooden theatres constructed in Rome by Scribonius Curio were placed back to back, so that after a play was shown in the morning, the two theatres could, through a mechanical device, be turned to face each other and form an arena to house gladiatorial fights. However, modern historians question the veracity of this account recorded by the historian Pliny (A.D. 23?–79). Still, Curio's two theatres must have been so unusual a structure that Pliny felt the need to write about it. That same year the great *naumachiae* (sea battles) were staged on the Fucine Lake east of Rome. Many of the nineteen thousand participants died, for the entertainment of the populace looking on from the shores. Amphitheaters were also flooded to simulate these events.

The few written dramas still to be seen at public festivals finally gave way to the increasing popularity of pantomime: individual actors performing the dramas, or parts of them, in a musical dance accompanied by a chorus speaking words from a truncated text. Considering the state of public taste, it is surprising that Seneca wrote any plays at all, as there was no longer an opportunity to have them produced except possibly in small private venues. This deterioration of Roman drama was documented by the Roman poet Horace (65–8 B.C.) in his *Ars Poetica* (24–20 B.C.?).

After Messalina was killed for the outrageous act of bigamy, Claudius' third wife Agrippina (also his niece as well as Julia's sister), interceded on Seneca's behalf, and he was recalled to Rome to tutor Agrippina's son, the future Emperor Nero. To secure her son the emperorship, in A.D. 54 Agrippina fed Claudius poisoned mushrooms. Claudius' son Britannicus, Rome's rightful heir, was also poisoned—probably by Nero. After the double murder, the seventeen year-old Nero ascended the throne, and Seneca became his chief minister in civil matters, managing to parlay this position into immense wealth. It is interesting that in both the Sophoclean and Senecan versions of the story, Creon's defense against Oedipus' charge of attempting a coup d'état, is that there is no motivation for him to do so, because he already benefits financially from his position as advisor without having the responsibilities of a ruler. Sophocles' Creon alludes to it; Seneca's Creon actually says he is given money for favors.

Seneca became Nero's most trusted advisor and for eleven years was at the heart of political power. But in A.D. 65 he was implicated in "Piso's Conspiracy" to assassinate Nero, and the twenty-eight-year-old Emperor commanded Seneca to kill himself. Ever the Stoic, Seneca attempted to do so with dignity by having the veins in his wrists slit open until he bled to death. There is some historical evidence, however, that like Rasputin, he did not die that quickly. According to Tacitus (A.D. 55?–120?), who wrote about it in his *Annals,* it took more than one attempt to kill him. When he didn't lose enough blood from the cuts in his wrists, he, like Socrates, reportedly drank a cup of hemlock. But the poisonous plant extract did not immediately kill him. He was then taken to a steam bath by Praetorian Guards where he eventually expired from suffocation. Though forbidden by Nero to make a will, his last request to be cremated was honored. As a result of the failed conspiracy, his two brothers and his famous nephew, Lucan, also committed suicide. Seneca's young second wife, Paulina, apparently survived Nero's wrath.

STOICISM

Second only to Cicero (106–43 B.C.) as a Roman philosopher, Seneca advocated the philosophy of Stoicism, which he learned by reading the works of early Greek philosophers such as Zeno of Citium (335?–265? B.C.), Cleanthes (331–232 B.C.), and Chrysippus (280?–207 B.C.). He also studied with Attalus, whom he refers to in *Epistle* CX.20. Seneca, like the early Stoics, believed that events are preordained, and human beings can only attain inner peace by calm acceptance of the unavoidable vicissitudes of divine will or natural order. "Whether fate holds us in bondage by rancorous law, or whether God as ruler of the universe has from the beginning orchestrated everything, or whether chance spins out human affairs without purpose or direction, philosophy must be our bastion." (*Epistle* XVI.5) The good life, he posited, is achieved through introspection, the suppression of emotion, the attainment of rational thought, and the shedding of material possessions. (Seneca's contemporaries took him to task for his immense wealth in light of his stoic beliefs.) But Seneca, espousing voluntary poverty, also posited that good Fortune—meaning material wealth—was a divine test of its recipient, and treated it as an evil temptation. Like Cicero, he did not protest against wealth, only against its abuse. For Seneca, to amass great wealth was not inherently selfish, provided it was used to help others. He defends himself against his accusers in *De vita beata*:

> The wise man does not consider himself unworthy
> of the gifts of Fortune. He has no love of riches, but
> he would rather possess them. He does not take them
> to his heart, but to his home, and he does not discard
> the riches he has; instead, he retains them hoping to
> supply others sufficient material for practicing his
> goodness. (*De vita beata*, XXI,4) *

He also taught that we must learn to endure pain and suffering, even death, with grace, dignity, and resignation—an accomplishment for which he strove and finally attained at the end of his life. "The power of philosophy to thwart the blows of chance is incalculable." (*Epistle* LVII.12)

---

* All translations of foreign texts are mine except where noted in Appendix II.

However, to the consternation of his followers, Seneca often quoted Epicurus (341–270 B.C.) who believed in the calm pursuit of happiness and pleasure (defined as the absence of pain), the attainment of mental serenity, the avoidance of wealth and power, and the end to one's fear of death through a deeper understanding of nature and science (atomic theory). Despite the rivalry of Epicureanism, Stoicism won widespread support in Imperial Rome because it was used to justify Roman imperialism and support the imperium as predestined, but it was Seneca who added a contemplative form of spirituality to what had originally been an austere, humanist philosophy.

GREEK AND ROMAN DRAMA

Judged an inferior dramatist by historians and scholars, Seneca's plays have been dismissed as long, abstruse, declamatory rhetoric—dramatically incompetent travesties of the Greek originals written for private recitations. In other words, unactable closet dramas not intended for stage performance and of less importance than other later examples of the genre such as Milton's *Samson Agonistes* (1671), Byron's *Manfred* (1817), or Shelley's *Prometheus Unbound* (1820). To attempt a modern production of a Senecan tragedy with its surfeit of barbaric, bloodthirsty decadence, its bombastic oratory, its obsession with horror, its maddeningly sententious aphorisms, is to encourage an exercise in futility. In fact, it has become traditional thinking since the early nineteenth century to laud the Greeks at the expense of the Romans. Because the Roman theatre has always been seen as a paltry imitation of the greater Greek theatre, it has been difficult to derive an accurate view of its strengths.

SENECAN DRAMATIC STRUCTURE

Seneca's *Oedipus* follows the Aristotelian unities of action and time. Though Aristotle (384–322 B.C.) did not discuss unity of place, the play also limits the action to one locale. This would have satisfied the Italian scholars of the sixteenth century—notably J. C. Scaliger, who in his own *Poetica* (1561) expressed rigid application of the so-called three unities. In fact, so pervasive was Seneca's influence on the Elizabethans (despite the devaluation of later critics), that every English schoolboy eventually read him in the original Latin—perhaps even Shakespeare, for it was he who made famous Seneca's maxim, "*Tanta stultitia mortalium est.*" ("What fools these mortals be…"). Shakespeare certainly gives credence to Seneca as the model for tragedy when in *Hamlet* he has Polonius say: "Seneca cannot be too heavy, nor Plautus too light." Revenge, horror, ghosts, and violent, bloody scenes became the staple of Elizabethan drama well into the seventeenth century. It was also Seneca's plays that convinced Renaissance dramatists to adopt the five-act structure. While an argument can be made that the five-act structure is the work of later editors, Horace in his *Ars Poetica* recommended its use. Seneca would have been familiar with Horace's writings, and no doubt incorporated his suggestion to divide plays into five episodes separated by choral interludes connected to the action. French critics of the seventeenth and eighteenth centuries approved of Seneca's five-act appropriation of the Greek plots, as did their most famous neo-classic playwright, Jean Racine (1639–1699). His tragedy *Phèdre*, though eschewing the stage violence of Senecan drama, combines the Stoic notion of fate with the notion of personal guilt much as Seneca uses it in *Oedipus*. Additionally, Racine's contemporary Pierre Corneille (1606–1684), and somewhat later Voltaire (1695–1778), wrote their own five-act versions of the Oedipus myth, Corneille in 1659, and Voltaire in 1718—both called *Oedipe*. Vittorio Alfieri (1749–1803), Italian playwright, novelist and poet, also used the Senecan model to dramatize ancient myths in order to condemn the oppression and tyranny of feudal lords.

Because Seneca's *Oedipus* is an adaptation of Sophocles' *Oedipus Tyrannus*, it ipso facto fulfills Aristotle's requirements for tragedy. That is, both plays embody Aristotle's definition of *anagnorisis* (recognition). *Anagnorisis* occurs when Oedipus realizes that he has killed his father, married his mother, and is responsible for the Theban plague. And like its predecessor, the Senecan play ends in Aristotelian *peripeteia* (a sudden reversal of situation) as the once mighty king blinds himself and abdicates the throne.

Though the plot in Seneca's *Oedipus* is essentially the same as Sophocles' *Oeidpus Tyrannus*, making his version as plot-driven as the original, the Senecan *Oedipus* is more than just another example of Aristotelian *Poetics* (c. 335 B.C.) in action. It is a play rich in verbal texture with grand images of mysticism and the occult that transcend the Aristotelian rules of tragedy. Its great tragic impact is accomplished through overriding mood. This dramaturgical technique is not unlike that used by the later Symbolists (1870s–1890s) who believed in "correspondences" between the physical and spiritual worlds, and aligned themselves with what was labeled as the "decadence" of Greek and Latin literature. Seneca's highly charged theatrical atmosphere, with the outcome no surprise, holds our attention by creating mounting visceral terror as it depicts impending doom. The atrocity at the end is the culmination and the climax of these tragic Roman dramas. And if his gory proto-symbolist plays have been deemed repugnant by history's critics, the plays perfectly reflect their stories, and are tame compared to the graphic bloodshed and horrid mutilation seen in contemporary film.

Though Seneca's Oedipus suffers (as does Sophocles') from too much *hubris* (pride), he is guilt-ridden and insecure about the plague. He feels, in some unknown way, that he is at fault, and from the beginning has a premonition of his tragic fate. We are not shocked by his fall. Not so with Sophocles. His Oedipus is arrogant, cocky, patronizing, and confident, certain he can put an end to the devastation. Yet, in each play, it is Oedipus' great moral stature, his *ethos* (character) that makes him a candidate for Aristotle's much-cited reversal of fortune. Seneca, like Sophocles, presents a noble Oedipus who possesses the same personality defect—intellectual pride, or *hamartia* (flaw), upon which the resolution and sudden shift in fortune of both plays depend. According to Aristotle, if the audience sees this change in fortune, it produces *catharsis*, or what the classical scholar, Leon Golden, calls "intellectual clarification" brought on by vicariously experiencing pity and fear. That is, pity for those onstage and fear for ourselves. Thus, at the moment of character insight comes a concomitant understanding in the audience. Conversely, Plato (427–347 B.C.) rejects *catharsis* because he thinks witnessing it makes men weak.

Unlike his teacher Plato, Aristotle sees *nemesis* (divine retribution) at the end of a tragedy as emotional purgation, not unhealthy stimulation; it makes us stronger for having experienced it. The argument is still unresolved and remains with us today whenever politicians and critics discuss the effects of television, film, or video game violence on audiences—especially children. Ironically, even though Oedipus wasn't Plato's definition of the philosopher-king, Plato would have appreciated the Senecan version, because it is closer to his own belief that the perceivable world is an illusionary shadow presenting natural phenomena as symbols of a greater transcendent realm leading to a higher degree of spiritual actualization. Plato believed we bring into this world time-transcending realities from a world inhabited prior to birth, and that these forces stick to us like the Delphic oracle did to Oedipus. Gilbert Murray (1866–1957), the classical scholar, also saw the connection between Plato and the Stoics when he wrote in his *Five Stages of Greek Religion*, "But the Stoics presently found themselves admitting or insisting that the same consensus proved the existence of daemons, of witchcraft, of divination, and when they combined with the Platonic school, of more dangerous elements still." Even Peter Brook, the great theatre director, in his latest book *Recollections* writes that "…what we call living is an attempt to read the shadows, betrayed at every turn by what we so easily assume to be real."

The seventeenth century metaphysical poets who used language to convey sense-impressions, and the mid-nineteenth century Transcendentalists who believed in a priori knowledge not derived directly from perception, would have agreed. Political writers have also begun to reexamine Seneca's theories. In the September 6, 1998 issue of *The New York Times Book Review*, Michael Lind, Washington editor of *Harper's* magazine, writes: "Cicero and Seneca meant far more to the American Founders than Plato or Aristotle." As example, in a letter dated October 31, 1819, Thomas Jefferson writes "Seneca is indeed a fine moralist, disguising his work at times with some Stoicisms, and affecting too much of antithesis and point, yet giving us on the whole a great deal of sound and practical morality." The traditional practice of looking backward to praise the Greeks at the expense of the Romans needs to be critically reappraised.

Seneca's Plays

Why read Seneca now? He's been out of favor for centuries. Obviously, it is because his nine plays plus *Octavia* are the only extant examples of Roman tragedy. But they have survived for reasons beyond offering *sententiae* (maxims) to be memorized by school children. Each age has found its own reflection in his plays. Our era is no exception. We now understand the meaning of plague in a way that was impossible before AIDS. Moreover, we have suffered two devastating World Wars, the Holocaust, ethnic cleansing, genocide, and the continued threat of nuclear annihilation. We can identify with those whose lives are filled with bitterness, despair, cynicism, and loss of faith. It is also not difficult to understand classical tragedy as a fall from a high place, because we have witnessed the tragic fall of one American president who suffered from the sin of pride.

Seneca dramatizes the unspeakable: incest, necromancy, sorcery, infanticide, patricide, vivisection, mutilation, and cannibalism—taboos common to the history of humankind. But his characters also display intelligence, persistence, courage, love, friendship, loyalty, and faith. True, there is much that is deeply disturbing about his brutal work, but it is honest because it dares to say that life gives you back exactly what it receives. Not exactly a comforting sentiment, but one we can live with in dignity, because according to Seneca, even if all life's wickedness is predetermined and the innocent suffer, it is still possible to confront this inscrutable force with fortitude and mercy.

Because his plays present lurid, violent, revolting, revenge-driven plots all taken from Greek mythology, and are filled with horror, psychological disassociation, and impending doom, their influence can be seen in modern writers from Edgar Allan Poe and H. P. Lovecraft, to Clive Barker and Stephen King. Obviously there is a modern audience who feels drawn to frightening subject matter beyond titillation, in that it seems to reflect what the postmodernists in our society say no longer exists: depth of feeling, meaningful simulacra, and coherent ideas.

Seneca offers more than vicarious rape, incest, murder, and mutilation to satisfy those with voyeuristic or prurient needs; his plays provide more than sensationalism for contemporary audiences. Our newspapers, television, films, and the Internet do a better job of that. And there is more here than stichomythia, or peroration. The plays offer ancient, tragic myths retold, but with introspective protagonists who try to cope with the same evils still flourishing today. As author and journalist Gilbert Keith Chesterton (1874–1936), in his book *Orthodoxy* says, "Thus the ancient world was exactly in our own desolate dilemma." Aleksandr Solzhenitsyn echoes this thought in his 1972 Nobel Prize acceptance speech:

> I think that world literature has it within its power
> in these frightening hours to help humanity know
> itself truly… in such a way that we will cease to be
> split apart and our eyes will no longer be dazzled …
> and some peoples may come to know the true history
> of others accurately and concisely and with that
> perception and pain they would feel if they had
> experienced it themselves—and thus be protected
> from repeating the same errors.

Unfortunately, contemporary critics have not embraced Seneca as having any relevance to the modern theatre beyond being an historical curiosity for creating mechanical and unmotivated, gory recitation pieces specifically designed for the entertainment of a depraved Roman audience. Such critics base their conclusions on a misconception of the actor/audience relationship of the time. A typical example of this kind of criticism is found in Clarence W. Mendell's *Our Seneca*. Mendell states that when Seneca has Oedipus speak his first long monologue on the stage with no one present (Sophocles has his Oedipus speak to the Chorus), it is "unmotivated recitation, a speech before the play begins, to put us in the proper mood." What Mendell fails to consider is that Oedipus is not alone; he talks to the audience. It is not a soliloquy—that poor stage device—in which a dramatic character reveals his private thoughts to an empty stage. The modern belief that characters in a classical play talked to themselves on stage is anachronistic. This erroneous idea comes from having seen too many renditions of "to be or not to be," directed as private soliloquies by theatre directors who do not understand that during the Elizabethan era, whenever characters were alone on stage, Shakespeare had them step forward to address the audience. Shakespeare, as did the other Elizabethan playwrights, simply followed Seneca's example and included the audience as part of the action.

These in-depth, audience-directed monologues represent the method Seneca used to create the more fully developed, introspective characters who stand as a bridge between the archetypes of ancient Greek drama, and the post-Freudian personae of the modern era.

GREEK VERSUS ROMAN TRAGEDY

It is generally accepted that the great Greek classical playwrights achieved their success because they grasped the ideas of exposition, development, complication, crisis, and resolution. They reasoned that character stems from plot, and that events need to be compressed for the stage. Seneca also understood these Aristotelian rules of dramaturgy. What made him take tragedy further is that he recognized there is more to experiencing pity and fear than creating a suspenseful plot. It is Seneca's unique ability to create a pervasive and claustrophobic mood hovering over his characters like a blanket of thick smoke, choking them and us with the pain of recognition—much like nuclear fallout after an exploded atom bomb, unstoppable devastation on its way, a modern god of vengeance visiting us on the wind—that gives his plays such modern relevance. (This inexorable force of destruction invading our lives is a major theme of the plays of Sam Shepard.) It is this apocalyptic vision that separates Seneca from the more stately Greek dramas. As recently as 1995, the English horror writer, Clive Barker, writes in his three-play anthology *Incarnations* that "claustrophobia is, of course, a common device in horror fiction, allowing the readers or spectators no escape from the source of their anxiety, and the theatre is arguably the easiest place to evoke it." Clearly, Seneca, regardless of his proclivity to offer stoic philosophy at every turn, is the progenitor of the modern horror story.

Imminent death is Seneca's unique means of dramatic foreshadowing. Fear of death is endemic and it is eternal. It has been written about since *The Epic of Gilgamesh.* Jeremy Taylor in his *The Rule and Exercise of Holy Dying* (1651) says "death reigns in all the portions of our time." We are always trying to elude death's grip as Oedipus did the Sphinx. The Buddhist philosopher Pandit Nagarjuna, who lived in India at about the same time Seneca lived in Rome, reasons in his commentaries called *The Staff of Wisdom* that "Life is held in the grinning fangs of Death." James, the half-brother of Jesus, and another contemporary of Seneca, comments that life is "a mist that appears briefly and then vanishes." (James 4:14)

In 1931, the Indian poet, symbolist playwright, and Nobel Prize winner, Sir Rabindranath Tagore (1861–1941) writes in *The Religion of Man,* "We have come to look upon life as a conflict with death...." Seneca, as so many of history's great writers and philosophers before and after him, sees life as an exquisitely intricate sand painting to be wiped away at any time by the sweep of fate's hand. It is this singular human knowledge that life must end, which gives it meaning. With the millenium around the corner, Dustin Hoffman in a television interview in May, 1999 put it this way: "We're very temporary. We're gone like that. In the best circumstances, we're all dying together." In *Epistle* LXI.4 Seneca concludes, "We must prepare for death before we can prepare for life." William Ernest Hocking in his *Thoughts on Death and Life* (1937) makes essentially the same point when he writes, "But to remain aloof is to die before one begins to live."

Can we be squashed by some supreme and unknowable force, our next door neighbor, or a stranger on a road, as easily and thoughtlessly as we step on a cockroach that accidentally crosses our path? Can a hidden bomb blow up in our face? Jocasta thinks so, as do the Existentialists. Death is always around the corner. It is this acute awareness of mortality that motivates Jocasta to plead with her husband to stop his search for Laius' murderer. She knows the discovery will destroy them. When the truth is exposed, when she has been shamed beyond redemption, she ends her life in a pool of her own blood. Seneca, more deeply than Sophocles, delves into human motivation to expose inner feeling. His characters are not archetypes; they are real people who, in the tradition of Euripides (480?–406 B.C.), feel as deeply and are as frightened and insecure as human beings can be.

Much of Creon's description of Tiresias' necromantic rite is written to provoke fear in the audience. His gruesome descriptions of the sacrificial place hidden from the light of day by overhanging trees, of pits resembling graves in which shrieking animals are burned alive, of ghosts rising up from the dead to threaten and curse Oedipus—all bring to mind the powerful Greek word *deisdaimonia* (fear of spirits), which Shakespeare used to name Othello's wife. But it is Seneca who comprehends its full meaning. If he is barbaric, it is because, more than any other classical playwright, he has consistently visited the darkest sides of humanity, the most hidden recesses of our psyche, and like Dante in Hell, has come back to describe its subterranean regions.

Yet, it is Seneca's language, probing the human soul, describing eerie events and otherworldly creatures, articulating the need to come to terms with the inevitable—not the integration of a well-conceived plot—that mesmerizes his audience, and gives his plays universal appeal. In the *Poetics* Aristotle sees placing the blame for Oedipus' tragic life on a personal character flaw. Seneca is concerned with creating an atmosphere of inexplicable, inevitable doom in which passion tragically wins out in a battle against reason. His interest is in our inability to avoid the vicissitudes and periodic horrors of fate responsible for so much human suffering. In *Open Minded*, Jonathan Lear puts it this way: "And—at least, from the ancient tragic perspective—fate is part of the basic fabric of the world. It is taken to be as fundamental an aspect of the world as we take gravity to be—only, unlike gravity, fate is impossible to defy."

Unlike Aristotle who, in exploring the nature of tragedy cites human imperfection as its cause, Seneca believes that human beings live at the whim of blind chance or divine will. He is not interested in placing blame for misfortune on human character flaws; he is interested in how we face a tragedy not of our own making. For Seneca, we may not always be in control of what happens to us, but we have the capacity to control how we respond to it. His central tenet is that we must try to find the strength to accept suffering with dignity, patience, and mercy. This philosophy seems as relevant today in a world filled with repeated horrors against those who are innocent, as it was in ancient times.

THE ADAPTATION

Seneca's long choral digressions can stand alone in the original Latin as lyric poems if one understands their allusions, because the syntax is pithy, clear, concise, and balanced. Unfortunately, these lyric arias tend to hold up the action. The challenge is to present a modern audience with a dramatic equivalent to these arcane choric songs by rendering into comprehensible alternatives what Frank Justus Miller, in the famous Loeb translations of Seneca, calls "allusions to points so abstruse as to puzzle the reader who is not thoroughly versed in mythology." Add to this issue the stilted early translations of the non-choric sections, and it is easy to see why Seneca has lost favor in the last two hundred years. The translations do not encompass or reflect his intense, grandiloquent speech, his phantasmagoric imagery, his unsurpassed probing of emotional pain; and they don't find modern equivalents to esoteric Greek mythology in ways that are accessible to a modern audience.

For instance, Seneca's second choral ode runs more than one hundred uninterrupted lines, touting the power of and the need to worship Bacchus, recounting his more familiar episodes with Pentheus and the Amazons turned into Maenads; but the ode also mentions Palaemon, the Bassarids, the Zalaces, the Gelonians, Naxos, Theseus, Jupiter, Ino, Nereus, and the Massagetes. It speaks of Silenus. Is our modern theatre audience expected to know that he was a satyr and Dionysus' tutor? Are we supposed to know on first hearing that Araxes and the Pactolus are rivers? Though Seneca's audience would have been familiar with both the mythology and the geography, he still could have improved the structure of his plays had he paid more attention to Horace, who wrote in the *Ars Poetica* that playwrights ought to move things along more quickly *in medias res* (in the midst of things), and not have the chorus sing tangential choral odes, which the modern translator E. F. Watling, in his introduction to the Penguin Classics edition of Seneca's *Four Tragedies and Octavia*, calls "for the most part flaccid and unconvincing."

Because of my belief that the Senecan plays were written for the stage—albeit a private one—and need only to be translated into understandable, contemporary, lyrical English to be appreciated, I have replaced the original abstruse choral odes with a character called Chorus who speaks to the audience directly from Seneca's moral philosophies, all of which are more accessible to modern audiences. These speeches have been culled and adapted from the misleadingly-named *Dialogi* (*Dialogues*), and the *Epistulae morales* (*Moral Letters*). Will Durant, in his *Caesar and Christ*, says of these epistles, "To read these letters is to be in correspondence with an enlightened, human, and tolerant Roman who has reached the heights and known the depths of literature, statesmanship, and philosophy. They are Zeno speaking with Epicurus' lenience and Plato's charm." (The specific sections of the epistles used for these new choral odes are listed in the Appendix I. A translation of the original choral odes is printed in Appendix II.)

The inclusion and juxtaposition of excerpts from these epistolary, moral essays purposefully disrupts the theatrical reality of the play, and offers a rational break from its unrelenting, passionate language. The Chorus periodically tones down the play's intensity with an appeal to the intellect instead of the emotions. This new Chorus also presents a model of Stoic restraint and dispassionate reasoning in contrast to the tragic loss of self-control experienced by Oedipus. The insertion of selections from Seneca's moral essays into the text of *Oedipus* offers an ideal opportunity to blend and harmonize what E. F. Watling refers to as "an astonishing incongruity between the humanity and dignity of the prose works and the bombastic extravagance, the passionate yet artificial rhetoric, of the tragedies." This technique might be best described as a post-Brechtian (1898–1956) *Verfremdungseffekt* (alienation effect), though it was also used by Rabindranath Tagore when he utilized a rhapsodist to comment on those portions of his plays presented in pantomime.

The selections are purposefully didactic, and positioned to shed light on the play's darkening tragedy by encouraging the audience to remain critically detached during these choric interpolations. John Gassner, the great American theatre critic, in an essay entitled "Aristotelian Literary Criticism," states that both empathy and objectivity exist in tragedy. He writes that "emotional involvement *and* detachment, 'pity and fear' *and* objectivity, are present in tragedy....." Gassner, like Brecht, discusses the need for "esthetic distance" in an effort to gain perspective about what we have just witnessed. In his essay "Catharsis and the Modern Theatre," Gassner suggests "that there can be no complete purgation for the spectator or reader without 'enlightenment' ensuing upon the 'pity and fear' he has experienced; and there can surely be no enlightenment concerning an experience that we cannot view from some emotional distance."

By enlightenment I do not refer to what the anticognitivists label as cognitive understanding. These critics connect cognition with pleasure, and then argue against it, citing Aristotle as giving little support for his theory in *Poetics* IV that learning is pleasurable. My intention here is not to refute or support anticognitive critics, but to create a dramatic structure out of the conviction that *catharsis* leads to insight, and that in order to achieve it, emotional distance is needed. Whether insight coincides with pleasure or pain depends on the individual who experiences it.

These moral essays spoken to us through the character of the Chorus, in their appeal to the mind rather than the heart, offer the audience an opportunity for emotional distance, a way station with time to reflect on what has transpired while on the road to achieving insight. Thematically, they challenge Oedipus' early unwillingness to accept personal responsibility; yet, they do not suggest we abrogate our responsibilities in a predestined world. On the contrary, the Chorus' philosophical talks to the audience advocate being held accountable for our actions regardless of how ill-fated they may seem, and not passively acquiescing to determinism. But most importantly, they remind us of our own mortality.

Still, certain portions of the original choral odes have been retained and enhanced, especially having to do with a description of the plague, or Seneca's brief mention of Daedalus. In the case of Daedalus, modern audiences may not be familiar with the story, but as its tragic conclusion bears a direct relationship to the fate of Oedipus, the new Chorus presents it more fully.

I have also put Manto's disembowelment of sacrificial animals offstage, and described her rituals in the past as if she has just come to tell of it. Rome's penchant for bloody stage events does nothing to further the action. On the contrary, slaughtering a real heifer or two on stage presents insurmountable problems both for the modern audience and the actors. Real blood onstage interferes with illusion, identification, and empathy. And it wouldn't have made any difference to Tiresias, who was blind. Either way, the ritual slaughter would have had to be described to him. Horace, too, suggests that violence and revolting deeds be kept off the stage, better described by a narrator. Regardless of its intention, the addition of Manto to the plot adds an intriguing sensuality not found in Sophocles, and is Seneca's unique invention.

I should also mention that I have restored parts of scenes left out of Seneca's version, but which are present in the original source, Sophocles' *Oedipus Tyrannus*. One such scene is Jocasta's return in Act II. In the Senecan version, Jocasta leaves at the end of Act I, and does not return until Act IV—too long a time for a major character to be off stage. In the Sophoclean play Jocasta attempts to mediate the argument between Creon and Oedipus. I have included this excerpt by bringing her back in Act III. I have also strengthened two other scenes between Jocasta and Oedipus, using material from the earlier play (which is very much in the tradition of the Plautine and Terentian practice of *contaminatio*), including the famous line "Many men before you have dreamt they shared their mother's bed." A further example is the altercation between Oedipus and Tiresias. Using material from Sophocles, it has been made into two scenes, one building on the other until Oedipus is finally exposed by Tiresias as the cause of the plague. In the Oedipus interrogation of the Herdsman I have restored the line "If what this man says is true and you are that boy, then no man living is more cursed than you." When the Herdsman leaves, Oedipus filled with self-loathing, like the biblical Jeremiah, curses the day he was born.

The most notable addition, however, is Creon's return at the end of the play, which seems necessary to resolve the play's action. It is easy to justify ending the play with Oedipus groping his way out of the city in self-imposed banishment, beckoning the plague to leave with him, hoping that with his departure a kinder spirit will watch over Thebes. But this resolution appears too open-ended, not quite returning things to order in Seneca's murky world of ghosts and magic. Sophocles prefers a greater degree of homeostasis. In his version, to mitigate the public's fear, Creon must return as the new king. Shakespeare also favors it when he has Fortinbras return at the end of *Hamlet*. Creon's entrance resolves Sophocles' *Oedipus* the way Malcolm, hailed as the new king, resolves *Macbeth*. In the Sophoclean version Oedipus asks Creon to banish him. Creon says it is up to the Gods, and ushers him back into the palace. Seneca has his Oedipus, unaided, blindly groping his way into exile. In this adaptation, I have combined both endings by having Creon lead Oedipus out of the city.

Yet, many critics feel the Senecan tragedy is as resolved as its Sophoclean predecessor without Creon's return. Indeed, most historians and theatre scholars believe that both plays end with the same supreme act of irony: Oedipus, accepting his fate, will return to the very slopes of Mount Cithaeron, his eye sockets pierced the way his infant ankle sockets were. The cycle is complete as he symbolically reverts to his original newborn state. But Seneca has something more encompassing in mind. He changes the wound from the ankles to the soles of the feet. The Latin *vestigia*, which means footprints, can also be used to indicate the part of the foot that produces footprints. Hence, *Forata ferro gesseras* **vestigia,** *tumore nactus nomen ac vitio pedium,* means "you had been born and had your soles pierced by iron, obtaining your name because of the swelling and subsequent defect in your feet." This is a particularly important line, because it strongly suggests that the Oedipus of Seneca is lame—a point glossed over in Sophocles. If one looks at lines 1031–1033 in *Oedipus Tyrannus* they only say:

OEDIPUS
What ailed me when you took hold of me?

MESSENGER
Your ankle sockets should tell you that.

OEDIPUS
Why do you bring up that childhood pain?

Nothing here indicates that Oedipus is lame or physically handicapped by his old wound. Having never seen a production where Sophocles' Oedipus limps, I would suggest that anyone interested in presenting the Senecan version of the myth consider it.

In accepting his Fate—he is blind *and crippled*, his wife dead, his kingship gone, replaced by Creon—Seneca's Oedipus stoically accepts inevitable change in what Nietzsche (1844–1900) later calls the "cycle of eternal recurrence." Tagore says it more poetically in his "The Four Stages of Life": "The flower must shed its petals for the sake of fruition, the fruit must drop off for the re-birth of the tree."

HISTORY OF THE SPHINX

A mythical creature of the ancient Middle East, it is portrayed in Egypt as a proud lion with a human head. This head is an idealized portrait of King Khafre, pharaoh of the Old Kingdom, who commissioned its construction in approximately 2500 B.C. This Great Sphinx was supposed to maintain order by divine rule in this world through his proxy image on earth as it guarded the pyramids of the ancient Giza necropolis. In Greek mythology, and in the Sophoclean *Oedipus*, the Sphinx sprouts wings and has the head of a woman. To the Greeks it seems to stand as a symbol of hidden, almost forbidden, knowledge. In the Senecan or Roman version it evolves into a hellish beast, intent on eating human flesh. From Egyptian through Greek to Roman mythology, the Sphinx changes from a symbol of benevolence to one of pure evil. From a royal guardian of order, insuring the safety of its people, and a vigilant keeper of the gateway between this world and the next, it becomes a demonic creator of chaos bent on destroying whomever comes near it.

What is, perhaps, even more interesting, is the actual history of its physical survival. The statue is massive, measuring two hundred and forty feet long and sixty-six feet high, three quarters the length of a football field, and the height of a six story building. By the time of the New Kingdom in Egypt, about 1570 B.C., the Great Sphinx was buried up to its neck in a thousand years of sand, and had to be extricated by order of King Tutmosis IV. When Alexander the Great conquered Egypt in 332 B.C., the Great Sphinx, again buried up to its neck in another thousand years of sand, had to be excavated once more.

Sometime after the death of Cleopatra in 30 B.C., the Roman conquerors led by Octavianus (soon to be titled Augustus) also repaired some of the scars and ravages of errosion. Each succeeding civilization has attempted to forestall its inevitable burial by sand. By the 1920s the Great Sphinx was again enveloped by sand. Its history, right to the present work on its excavation and restoration, has been that of repeated deaths and resurrections—a theme in Seneca's *Oedipus* that begins this adaptation. Chorus, quoting from Seneca's *Ad marciam*, XXVI. 6-7, refers to an apocalypse that is similar to early Christian theology when he predicts that "Whenever God sees fit to restore our world…when all things cool down again…We…being only a small accessory to the universal ruination…shall be returned to our former elements."

While both Sophocles and Seneca refer to the Sphinx's riddle, neither playwright presents the enigma verbatim. Presumably, Greek and Roman audiences were familiar with it, so that it was unnecessary to do so, but modern audiences may not be as well-versed. Hence, I have included the fatal question and its answer in this version of the play.

THE PLAGUE

It is generally accepted that Greek tragedy has its birth in the choric dithyramb honoring Dionysus. The origins of Roman drama are more controversial. If we believe Livy's history, Roman drama began when Etruscan mimetic dances were introduced in Rome around 364 B.C. as a reaction to a plague. Livy (59? B.C.–A.D. 17) writes, "the plague lasted this and the following year…and when neither human learning nor the help of Heaven was found to relieve the scourge, men abandoned themselves to irrational fears, and in addition to other efforts to assuage the anger of the gods, are said to have introduced scenic entertainments." (*History of Rome*, Book VII, ch.2)

Curiously, the inciting action of Sophocles' play is also the arrival of a plague, but here its purpose is to set into action the fall of a king because of personal weakness. Sophocles devotes approximately nine lines of the first choral ode to its description. Seneca, in contrast, uses both Oedipus' first speech and the first choral ode to create more than 160 lines graphically describing the ghastly effects of this deadly sickness, and comes much closer to depicting the realistic horror of it.

Throughout Western history the plague has had its chroniclers. The Greek historian Thucydides (471?–400? B.C.) wrote about it; Giovanni Boccaccio (1213–1375) penned a work of fiction based on The Black Death of 1348, which swept through Europe and parts of Asia, and is reported to have wiped out three quarters of the population in a twenty-year period. The English diarist Samuel Pepys (1633–1703) reported on the plague of 1665, as did Daniel Defoe who turned the event into fiction. Not until the beginning of the eighteenth century did the threat of plague abate, but its horror has left its descendents with a built-in fear that has lasted for centuries. In our own time Albert Camus (1913–1960) based a novel on the fictitious plague of Roan. So powerful a symbol is the plague, and so catastrophic its impact, that graphic descriptions of its devastation run through The Old Testament and The New Testament from Genesis to Psalms to Revelations. In Revelations, there is a plague of giant locusts described as having human faces, lion's teeth, wings, scorpion tails, and women's hair—eerily similar to descriptions of the sphinx found in ancient mythology. From beginning to end, the Bible attests to its ferocity as a display of God's wrath. Ironically, from Sophocles to Seneca to the present day, writers have used the plague either as a symbol of divine retribution, or as an example of a godless universe run by chance.

MUSIC

Though little is known about musical accompaniment during the Roman period, there are references to the use of a flute player with a wooden instrument made of two tubes about twenty inches long with finger holes, and tied to the musician's head, so as to keep his hands free to cover the stops, moving about the stage accompanying one character or another. Horace calls for its use, but only in a simple and unembellished mode. Horace may have made this comment as a reaction against the emerging practice of using flutes, pipes, and cymbals for the new pantomimes. While I do not recommend adding a flute player to the dramatis personae of *Oedipus*, incidental woodwind music of a plaintive style, utilizing both a flute and oboe, would enhance the play's haunting and evocative atmosphere. Combining the primal sound of the wooden flute with the richer timbre of the modern oboe connects the past with the present, the primitive with the modern, thus reflecting the play's antipodal forces as well as producing consonance that more closely approximates the ancient flute. They become the musical equivalent of *Eros* and *Thanatos* (life and death), pulling at Oedipus the way "Solomon's child" was pulled in opposite directions by two women until the real mother, seeing the child's pain, relinquished her hold. Tagore once said that his plays could only be understood if they were listened to as one would listen to the music of the flute.

PRODUCTION

Similar to the plays themselves, virtually all Roman theatre architecture is a modification of the earlier Hellenistic period of Greek theatre design. And as was true of the ancient Greek theatres, dramatic events were first housed for the most part in temporary wooden structures. Unlike the Greek theatres they imitated, they were not built into hillsides, but on level ground. The great Roman exception, the theatre of Ephesus in what is now Turkey, was built into a hillside in the third century B.C. It was remade in stone during the first century A.D. for gladiatorial combats, and seated 24,000 spectators. Its *cavea* (auditorium) was built into the hillside's natural incline. Unlike their Greek prototypes, temporary theatres were demolished after each festival. The largest temporary theatre the Romans ever built, according to Pliny the Elder (A.D. 23?–79), was three stories high supported by three hundred and sixty columns. The first level was made of marble, the second level glass, and only the top level of wood. Built in 58 B.C., it held eighty thousand spectators. Like the others, the theatre was torn down after it had served a particular occasion.

It was not until 55 B.C. that the first permanent Roman stone theatre was erected. It was called the Theatre of Pompey, and held by some estimates as much as forty thousand people. The Romans built, perhaps, as many as 125 permanent outdoor stone theatres throughout their empire, some of which can still be seen in places as far from Rome as the Theatre in Caesarea, Israel (where many Jewish prisoners—like Christians in the Colosseum—were killed in combat with wild beasts); the larger Theatre of Orange in France whose acoustics are world renowned; the grandiose Theatre of Mérida in Spain; the Theatre of Timgad (preserved by desert sands) in Algiers, and the previously mentioned theatre of Ephesus in Asia Minor. Most accommodated from five to as many as forty thousand patrons.

These exquisite adaptations of Hellenistic theatres had rising tiers of semicircular, stadium seats, which were formally arranged. The first fourteen rows surrounding the *orchestra* (semicircular dancing space in front of the stage) were reserved for the senatorial order. Behind them sat members of the equestrian order; and behind them, in the largest section of the huge half-circle, sat the plebeian class. For officials presiding over the event, there would be special box seats at the side and front close to the orchestra. In imitation of the ancient Greek theatre, in which all action was played on ground level in front of the *skene*, some stage action was played on the semicircular *orchestra*, but the major action happened on a long wooden, raised *pulpitum* (stage) that spanned the width of the stadium seating. Like the Greek theatre, it included a *scaena frons* (building with dressing rooms), which the actors could also use for exits and entrances, as well as the backdrop for scenery; still, it was much larger than the Greek version, which was only as wide as their circular *orkhestra* (also dancing space). Unlike the Greek *skene*, this building had an extended roof that covered the stage and protected its façade. It also improved the theatre's acoustics. At the sides of these stages both the Romans and the Greeks used *periaktoi* (triangular rotating modules) that displayed a painted tragic, comic, or satyric scene—depending on the play presented. Scenes were also depicted on *proskenia* (pedestals with decorations in relief).

While the Romans did possess the machinery to move and lift heavy stage properties, a further discussion of these permanent theatres is moot, because no surviving historical document mentions Seneca's plays having ever been presented in these public, stone amphitheaters.

As has been stated, Roman audiences became more interested in public spectacles, special effects, and sensationalism, which had a deleterious effect on the production of tragedies in the large stone theatres of Rome. (In our own time, much the same can be said of present-day action films and spectacular Broadway musicals.) Consequently, I have taken the position that since there was no longer any opportunity to present tragic drama publicly, and because of Seneca's close connection to Nero, *Oedipus* was written to be presented privately, at the palace in costume, to the Roman senatorial order and their families. This view is strengthened if one compares the opening of the Sophoclean play, which has Oedipus publicly addressing the city's elders on the steps of the palace, to the Senecan version. Seneca's Oedipus considers the same subject, but it is his wife who first responds to him, not the city elders. With the exception of one line introducing Creon's entrance, the Senecan chorus does not participate until three scenes and four hundred lines have elapsed. The opening event is of a more intimate nature—a scene between husband and wife. Therefore, I have placed it and the play *within* the palace instead of on its steps as indicated in the Sophoclean account. Both plays begin with a discussion of the plague—one public, the other private.

Audiences today are used to relatively small regional theatres across the country, all of which allow for greater proximity between actor and audience. Certainly, the major dramatic entertainment of our present age is film, which permits an even greater degree of intimacy between performer and viewer. To try to produce a Roman tragedy in the middle of say, a contemporary sports arena, would indeed be foolhardy. It is for these reasons that I have devised this particular adaptation as happening not in the public arena, but privately within the palace interior, so that the audience can be brought as close as possible to the live actors.

MASKS

Masks were used to portray different characters in the ancient Greek theatre. They were also used in the same way from the inception of the Roman theatre. Lucian (A.D. 125–190), the Syrian-Greek satirist, mentions that the masks of tragedy, which were made of linen and included a high hairdress (usually referred to by the Greek term *onkos*) that covered the entire head, were more exaggerated than the more natural-looking masks of comedy. Their use allowed for doubling of characters and enabled men more convincingly to portray women, who were not permitted to act on the stage. Quintilian (A.D. 35?–95?), the famous Roman teacher of rhetoric, mentions that some masks had two sides: comic and serious. An actor could reverse his stance if he wanted to portray the opposite emotion. There are also extant terracotta reliefs, mosaics, lamps, wall paintings from Pompeii, marble medallions, statuettes—all depicting Roman actors using full face masks. One wall painting showing actors wearing masks was discovered in a columbarium in the Villa Doria-Pamphili in Rome. It now resides in the Museo Nazionale

Romano delle Terme. In the same museum there is a tragic scene on a terracotta relief found in a tomb monument from Via Salaria. It, too, displays actors in full masks. The masks were arranged on shelves in order of appearance (as drawn in the Terence manuscripts housed in the Vatican), so that actors could easily change them as they switched characters. The tragic masks were apparently so frightening that, according to Lucian, one audience in Spain fled a performance in fear for their lives. This type of horrific mask was already out of fashion by the time Seneca wrote his plays.

The change began when women began to perform in mimes beginning in the first century B.C. The subject of many of these new mimes was adultery, and were immediately more popular than the masked plays. Because facial expression was so integral a part of the mime, and men no longer had to play the part of a woman, all masks for this type of entertainment were discarded. Mime became so prevalent a form of theatrical entertainment, it eventually replaced tragedy in the theatre. Since tragedy was no longer presented at the public theatres, and only mime seemed to please the populace, the terrifying masks were put aside. Mime led to the development of pantomime in 22 B.C., which led to a resurgence in the use of masks because women did not perform in them, as a single male actor played all the roles. Now using a closed-mouth mask, the actor told the story through dance, while a chorus narrated the story. Orchestral music was used to accompany these events. At first the pantomimes were also comic, poking fun at the amorous side of Olympic society, but they quickly developed into serious pieces dramatizing the lives of such tragic figures as Medea, Phaedra, Hercules, and Oedipus. Because these pantomimes appealed to the more cultured taste, they were done at funerals, or in a private stage setting for the upper classes. It is possible that Seneca, still seeing the need for tragedy, used a private setting for his aristocratic plays; one that would have made it easier for his actors to achieve a more realistic acting style closer to our own. Seneca says the following about actors:

> Actors in the theatre can imitate the emotions,
> portray anxiety and dread, depict grief, imitate
> shyness by hanging their heads, lowering their
> voices, and keeping their eyes fixed on the ground,
> but they are unable to conjure up a blush; for the
> blush cannot be prevented or acquired. (*Epistle* XI.7–8)

This comment would suggest that Seneca had seen actors perform without masks, and may have taken advantage of the audience's preference for seeing the expressive face of an actor, rather than a mask with a fixed image. Moreover, traditional Roman masks, designed to play to as many as forty thousand people, would have looked grotesque in a small and intimate setting.

Nevertheless, I recommend that certain characters still wear a simple, half-mask at specific moments in the play. Specifically, the Chorus wears the mask when he becomes a medium through which the Gods speak; other times he speaks without it; Manto wears her mask when she is in a shamanistic trance describing the mutilation of sacrificial animals, and Oedipus wears a mask after he has blinded himself, symbolizing his spiritual atonement for personal sin.

Since acting in an outdoor stadium with full face masks meant performing with exaggerated gestures and declamatory acting not acceptable to a modern audience, this adaptation is placed in a private and intimate setting; therefore, no attempt to stylize the acting should be made even when wearing the half-mask. Actors presenting this play should approach it as realistically as they would any contemporary play. It is maddening enough to watch today's opera singers perform with little concern for the acting. Apparently, Horace feels similarly. In his *Ars Poetica* he complains that Roman actors have become artificial and rhetorical. If the contemporary actor's passion is great, and the emotions true, Seneca's language will soar above today's prosaic texts without sounding like declamation, and Horace will finally be satisfied.

STAGING

It should be noted that the corpus of Senecan tragedy survives only in medieval manuscripts that do not contain any stage directions. There are no indications as to how or where they may have been produced. Consequently, the presentation of any Senecan tragedy must rely on a few wall paintings, some inference from bare texts, and the director's intuition.

When the Department of Theatre at Hunter College of the City University of New York sponsored the world premiere of this version of Seneca's *Oedipus*, I chose to set the play in a post-holocaust future. It seemed to me that this far distant world would create enough separation from a contemporary audience, so that the heightened language would be accepted as indigenous to that culture. Audiences used to seeing post-apocalyptic films could relate to the concept of vast destruction, and they could relate to the plague as reflective of our own time. This concept also seemed consistent with Seneca's own era, in that he lived during that period when many apocalyptic texts circulated throughout Rome. Imminent devastation was the directorial metaphor, inspired by the real and perennial threat of a sudden nuclear attack, and consistent with Seneca's theme of impending doom.

The setting was an underground royal bunker complete with decontamination chamber, temporarily protecting its inhabitants from the encroaching new holocaust. Characters who came and went wore protective masks and gear to show that the outside air was contaminated. All had recondite facial and body tattoos and some body-piercing; the king had a shaved head recalling the concentration camp prisoners of World War II. Most royalty sported crimson, blue or magenta hair, wore clothes made of luminous, metallic-looking plastics, and carried laser weapons instead of swords. The underground royal bunker echoed those places in our history where ordinary citizens stock-piled provisions and voluntarily shut themselves in not to be seen again until the plague ran its course. It was to look like a futuristic bomb shelter that had been converted from an ancient catacomb, as if Oedipus and his retinue were symbolically buried alive. It represented my vision of a stone fortress in hell. The vault is in contrast to, yet a reminder of the confinement of hoards of people in our annals who were locked in their houses against their will by local orders of quarantine, not only to perish because of the disease, but also for lack of food, water, and decent hygiene. Sadly, those who did break out often spread the plague even further. From a directorial point of view, the concept was to use the known past as an unsettling harbinger of things to come, and to use the intimacy of the Loewe Theatre to make the audience feel like inhabitants of this underground fortress whenever Chorus addressed them.

For directors and designers interested in a less oracular approach to the play, *Oedipus* can be presented as if it were a private presentation for the intelligentsia of Nero's Rome, using what was probably the natural architecture of the Imperial Roman throne room. Nero loved the theatre, and we know he attended the few *fabula togata* still being performed publicly, because contemporary sources refer to a stage building in a play entitled *House on Fire* by Lucius Afranius that was burned on the stage to his hearty applause. Nero also thought of himself as Rome's greatest actor. As his tutor and closest advisor, it is a valid assumption that Seneca wrote *Oedipus* so that the emperor could play the part of Oedipus at a private palace showing. According to Suetonius (A.D. 69?–140), in addition to playing gods, Nero also played Oedipus, Heracles and Orestes. (*Nero,* X, XXI, XLVII). Margarete Bieber, in *The History Of the Greek and Roman Theater,* writes: "Seneca may also have inspired his pupil Nero to give tragic recitations on the stage." Bieber goes on to say that "At these occasions he [Nero] must have worn the tragic costume in the form depicted in the wall paintings of his period." There are two contemporary wall paintings from Casa del Centenario in Pompeii that *may* depict scenes in full costume from Seneca's *Oedipus* or *Heracles* as well as one from *Medea.* It is possible that *Oedipus* could have been presented within the palace at a private, costumed performance for the edification and entertainment of Rome's aristocracy. For those interested in presenting the play in this manner, I have outlined a possible setting:

> The performance takes place in the Roman Imperial throne room during Nero's reign. Historically, the throne room was located between the halls of religion and justice, with archways to them from stage left and stage right. Though the original throne room was rectangular, the preferred effect here is that of a rotunda.

> The room's ceiling is semi-domed, with evidence of the Roman arch and vault. A richly patterned, tiled, mosaic floor is relieved by veined marble columns of the Corinthian order all around the room. They line up along the walls, separating individual niches that display art. These columns are connected by tapestries that open and close. Upstage center there is a large, formidable double-door of forged metal with the raised Imperial Seal of Nero on it. Both sides swing open revealing an inner courtyard housing the royal gardens. Above the door is a large, semicircular window divided in equal panes through which sunlight enters the room.

On each side of the door is a large niche with a
full-length painted, marble statue brought back
from conquered Greece. Both statues are different
versions of Aphrodite, such as the "Aphrodite of
Capua," and the "Callipygian Aphrodite." The
statues are nude and only partially draped.

The throne, which sits on a large, raised, two-stepped,
marble platform is just right of center stage, and at
an angle to the audience. It is the most dominant
scenic element in the room. A gold half-face mask
rests on the throne, its vacant eyes staring out at
the audience.

On the upstage side of the throne stands a bronze
candelabrum that is practical. To the right of the
throne on the down right wall there is a smaller niche
with a life-size bronze bust of Augustus Caesar in it.
The stage left wall is decorated with a large Roman
wall painting like the "Myth of Ixion," found in the
ruins of Pompeii, or the "Tragic Actor After the Agon,"
from the *Herculaneum*, a small Roman theatre in
the provinces. Both show depth, shade, shadow
and reflected light. Under the wall painting is an
intricately carved, large ebony chair with ivory legs
and a medium-high, curved back. On either side of
the chair stand two candelabra. These are also used to
light the room for night scenes and should be practical.

One final note to conclude a rather long introduction.
Whether a production of this play is seen as a futuristic piece,
or an historical recreation of the Roman era, presenting it as an
example of a more introspective Oedipus in an apocalyptic
drama will separate it from Greek tragedy. Seneca's *Oedipus* is
not a pallid imitation of Sophocles. It represents a vision of the
world present during the age within which Seneca lived. Ju-
daic/Christian apocalyptic literature initially appeared around
250 B.C., and continued into the early centuries A.D. Its
eschatological symbols run through both the Old Testament
and the New Testament from the book of Daniel to the book of
Revelations, offering comfort and the promise of salvation for
the faithful in times of crisis, persecution, famine, war, and
plague. Apocalyptic themes express hope for a world replete

with evil, which God will one day destroy, setting the stage for exultation, prosperity, and justice to reign in the new millennium. Seneca, in *Epistle* CII.28, reflects this view when he says, "someday the secrets of heaven will be revealed to us, and all our ignorant darkness will be dispelled by glorious light." I've chosen to end *Oedipus* with that image, because it is as relevant to our age as it was to his.

What follows is a free adaptation of Seneca's *Oedipus* written to be performed as a full stage production, the time and place left to the imagination of those producing it.

Michael Elliot Rutenberg
Boca Raton, Florida
1999

✸   ✸   ✸

O E D I P U S

VERITAS SIMPLEX ORATIO EST

TRUTHFUL LANGUAGE IS SIMPLE

Seneca
Epistle XLIX

DRAMATIS PERSONAE

❂   ❂   ❂

IN ORDER OF APPEARANCE

CHORUS
Roman philosopher and statesman

OEDIPUS
King of Thebes

JOCASTA
Queen of Thebes

CREON
Brother to Jocasta

TIRESIAS
A blind prophet

MANTO
Tiresias' daughter

CORINTHIAN VISITOR

OLD HERDSMAN

PALACE GUARD

THE TRAGEDY IS IN FIVE ACTS.

ACT ONE

❂ ❂ ❂

SETTING

The Imperial throne room in Rome during Nero's reign. Double bronze doors with an overhead, semi-circular, variegated window, leading to the royal gardens. Archways stage left and right leading offstage to the halls of justice and religion respectively. All scenic elements and costumes are Roman with the exception of two Greek statues of Aphrodite. Opulence and magnificent decoration are paramount, yet there is a cold beauty to this room, possibly because of the intricately carved stone chairs, tile floors, and many marble columns.

One stone chair with a low back is in the first row center of the audience. It is for CHORUS *to sit in when he is not on stage.*

AT RISE

Enter CHORUS *from the upstage center double-doors. He closes them. Outside it is gray dawn. He wears sandals and is dressed in the heavily draped, white toga of the period. He sees the audience, picks up a gold half-mask resting on the throne, and steps forward to speak to them.*

CHORUS
I'm glad you've come.
It's important to know there'll be witnesses.
Whenever there's a special occasion,
    we Romans always seem to feel
    the need for an audience
        to make the event official.
It's our grand compulsion,
    carried over from the Greeks.
They, too, were big on community participation.
Which brings me to the story you are about to see
    —the tragedy of Oedipus.

It's Greek…
The same as those two magnificent statues
    our noble generals appropriated
    for the greater beauty of Rome,
        as well as the better preservation of antiquities.

The plain truth is we Romans
    can't sculpt as well as they did.
I particularly detest our death masks.
Apparently ugliness isn't a concern to public taste,
    as long as the face is strong.

So, we surround ourselves with other people's art.
In fact…
    it's become the current rage:
Foreign art everywhere you look.

But that bust over there is authentic Roman…
And a pretty fair resemblance to Caesar Augustus.
That recent wall painting is also Roman.
Our artists… it seems…
    are further along with the brush than the chisel.
So there's hope for immortality.
Though we Romans must someday die, our art may live on.

However, as I am the Chorus in this tragedy,
    and not an art critic,
I'll confine my comments to a prediction
    given strictly in the spirit of the play.
Here's the prophecy…

[*He puts the mask on.*]

When the time shall come
    for the world to end…
All the forces of Nature
    will perish in conflict with each other.
The stars will dash themselves together,
    and all the heavenly lights
    will burst in one cataclysmic inferno.

Then we… the souls of the departed…
    and the heirs of our history…
Whenever the gods see fit to restore our world…
    when all things cool down again…

We...
> being only a small accessory to the universal ruination...
> shall be returned to our former elements.

I'll talk to you again,
> as the events of this tragedy unfold.

> [*He removes the mask, carries it with him, and goes to his seat in the audience. Enter* OEDIPUS *wearing the Imperial purple wool mantle, embroidered with gold threads worn over a toga and tied at the neck. He has on high-laced sandals.* JOCASTA *is with him. She is dressed in a diaphanous pastel tunic, stola and palla, which is attached to a diadem. The effect is more flowing than transparent. She wears gold, jewels, and a diamond brooch. He wears a garland, sheathed sword and belt.*]

OEDIPUS

This insufferable night is almost at its end.
The morning sun
> begins to show its hesitant face.

It drags itself out
> from behind some silent ominous cloud,
> and stares unwillingly at the sick earth below,
> bringing with it gloom instead of hope.

Beneath it our streets and homes,
> our temples—all glutted with the plague.

New heaps of dead spewed up everywhere,
> stiffening in the sickly morning light.

The brightening day to reveal...
> all too soon...
>> the carnage night has brought.

Before this evil plague besieged my city
> our people were happy.

Now there is disaster everywhere.
I don't understand
> why the gods have done this to us.

I stopped the hideous Sphinx.
Answered the riddle.

Destroyed her utterly.
And for that... as custom required...
> I was made king and husband to you,
> their widowed Queen.

And now this stinking pestilence
    has struck a second time,
    spreading havoc throughout the land,
    making me think that...
    I may be—in some unknown way—
    responsible for this catastrophe.

I feel at this very moment,
    the Fates are planning
    some savage stroke against me.
What else should I think
    when the blight that ravages Thebes
    seems only to spare me
    and those closest to me.
For what punishment am I reserved
    that I remain unscathed amidst the devastation
    that lays waste to everything in its path?

The city is in ruins.
No section of the populace has escaped its deadly touch.
It is obvious that unknowingly I have sinned,
    or the gods would not wish to wreck my kingdom.
Look around you.
Have you been outside?
Beyond the palace nothing grows.
The harvests stand ruined.
Springs have dried up
    and turned to stinking pools that reek of death.
The stench of rotting corpses is everywhere.
There isn't time any longer for a proper burial.
Instead... pile upon pile of diseased bodies
    are heaped upon the funeral pyres and set ablaze.
Tearless relatives watch their once loved families
    go up in billowing black smoke,
    wondering when they'll be next.

It seems we all await the funeral pyre.
I should pray for a quick, merciful death.
I don't want to survive to the last...
    the final witness to the end of Thebes.

JOCASTA

Sweet husband,
    why do you wish to make your misery more wretched
        by lamentation?

Confront adversity.
The darker the calamity, the firmer you must stand.
You are the king—
 not some baby crying in the night for mother's milk.
It is cowardly to turn your back on Fate and want to die.

OEDIPUS

I am no coward.
I would stand against the rage of Mars himself.
Did I run from the gnashing fangs of the ravenous Sphinx?
I faced that screeching beast,
 though her drooling, snapping jaws
 dripped succulently in anticipation of another
  human meal.
There she sat...
 perched upon her ugly, jagged rock
 while all around her on the ground
 lay bleached bones picked clean.
Waiting... with lashing tail and massive outspread wings,
 the monstrous lion sat, her quivering mouth
 eager to gorge herself on unsuspecting prey.
But I stood fast and asked: "What is your riddle?"
 that I may answer—
 and in so doing, freely enter this great city
 you so zealously guard.
She clawed and nearly split the rock,
 her talons impatient to rip out my heart.

Through teeth sharpened on human bones,
 the creature asked her fatal question.
Out of that baited trap shrieked sounds so horrible
I thought my ears would burst:
  "What is it that has four legs at dawn...
  two legs at noon...three legs at dusk...
  and is weakest when it has most?"
      her disgusting screech demanded.
The answer came to me in a flash.
'Man,' I said.
'A baby crawls on all fours... an adult walks on two...
 an old man uses a cane,
 and is weakest when he has most.'

Hearing the answer,
 she flapped her wings frantically up and down
 and began to writhe.

Her body shook, smashing itself against the pointed rock.
Her jaws clashed together, biting at the empty air
    until blood streamed from that fetid mouth.
Finally, with one last piercing scream,
    The beast convulsed and toppled from its craggy perch,
    to lie forever silent among the bones around her.

JOCASTA

Oedipus…
    you came to us ten years ago,
    a stranger from another land,
        and liberated our city from the dreaded Sphinx.
You can do it again.
This is a new riddle to solve.
Thebes calls you its savior because of what you did.
The gods will protect you,
    otherwise why have they let you live till now?
I beg you… don't turn away from Thebes.
Help us. You brought fortune with you once.
It can happen a second time.
No one questions your power to rule.
But rule men, not a city of corpses.
An empty ship… an abandoned city…
    are no more than ashes after a fire.

When I carried and bore our children
    it was to pass on to them a great kingdom
    and a life filled with future hope.
When I spread my legs and squat,
    the blood that flowed from my womb to the ground
        at each of their births,
    was to signal life, not death.
They must live… our children must live… Don't abandon them.
You wear the kingly garland,
    that crowning glory signifying battle won
        against the wingéd beast.
Use that power the gods have given you.
You can stop the plague
    the way you stopped the Sphinx.

OEDIPUS

That damned beast is not dead.
I killed her body,
    but her festering spirit hovers like a cloud of doom,
    smothering us with its stench.

I see only one hope left,
    to send your brother Creon to the oracle of Apollo
    to learn what must be done to rid us of this curséd plague.
He is a sober, rational man whose wisdom I admire.
If Apollo sends a sign,
I would sooner trust Creon's judgment
    than my own court prophets.
He is a faithful brother to us
    and of great help to me in matters of state.
We will find a way to put an end to this unending devastation.

JOCASTA

After you speak with him,
    come lie with me awhile
        before the morning air becomes too stifling
        with the smell of death.
There is nothing more to do till his return.

> [*Exeunt* OEDIPUS *and* JOCASTA.
> CHORUS *leaves his seat, dons his mask,*
> *walks to the stage, and speaks to the*
> *audience.*]

CHORUS

The plague began with the sheep.
There was death in the grass upon which they grazed.
In the fields the animals lay abandoned.
The herdsmen dead...
    together with the sickened herd and stinging viper,
        whose lethal venom had dried up within its shriveled skin.

Soon everything green withered,
    and the woods,
        whose leafy folds once cast cool shadows across the land,
          stood like blackened skeletons
          signaling the end was near.
On silent farms
    human bones remained within their cloaks.
Skulls lay on plague-polluted pillows.
Death had opened its greedy mouth to consume them all.

Some said it was the hound itself
    come up from Hades to set its demons on them.
All waited in terror for the inevitable moment—
    the first irreversible sign:

The legs weaken and go limp…
Red pustules appear upon the skin…
    open and ooze their purulent filth.
Burning, rushing fever swells the body.
Black blood bursts through the mouth and nose.
The eyes no longer see.
Scores thrash blindly about
    until they find and hug cool stones along the river bank
        to try in vain to quench the raging fever.

Finally, they crowd the temples
    blindly groping for a place across the sacrificial altars
        to stay and pray for death—
        the one prayer the gods were quick to grant.

[He returns to his seat.]

ACT TWO

It is now noon. CREON *enters and waits.*
A moment later OEDIPUS *enters from the*
opposite side.

OEDIPUS
Creon! Do you bring news of our salvation?

CREON
The god at Delphi does not speak so simply.
He couches his prophesies in enigmas.

OEDIPUS
All oracles are ambiguous. It is part of their nature.
Repeat exactly what you heard.

CREON
The oracle is dark and uncertain.

OEDIPUS
I will hear it without further delay.

CREON
It is Apollo's custom to trap us in his secrets.
Be wary.

OEDIPUS
I will have no more of this procrastination, brother.
Say what you heard.

CREON
Apollo's instructions are:
        the murder of King Laius be avenged.
That the assassin lives amongst us fed and cherished,
        and must be banished before the air in Thebes
                returns to purity,
                and the plague abates.

OEDIPUS
King Laius?
The noble monarch who ruled before me?

CREON

Yes, Oedipus.

OEDIPUS

I never saw the man.
As you know…
    the throne was empty when I arrived.
Did Apollo reveal the assassin's name?

CREON

I will tell you what transpired when I approached
    the shrine at Delphi.
You know the place.
You've prayed there many times.

I prepared myself properly,
    purified my body and entered the holy cave,
    my head bowed in supplication,
        when suddenly the twin peaks of mount Parnassus
        began to quake.
The ground under me trembled,
    and the Castalian spring began to boil.
Apollo's priestess—who was ahead of me—took to a fit,
    writhing and rolling on the buckling ground.
Then a voice,
    louder than any human one,
        roared out of her
        and filled my ears until I thought my head would split.

OEDIPUS

What did you hear?
I will submit to Apollo's command.

CREON

"Health and prosperity shall return to Thebes when
our murderous guest (known by Apollo from birth)
no longer pollutes the city with his presence."
She said something else, but I did not understand it.

OEDIPUS

Continue. I will hear it all.

CREON

The oracle said the murderer has returned
    to his mother's womb.

OEDIPUS
It is not difficult to interpret.
The killer was born here
    and has recently returned to his place of birth.
He will be found and banished.
But it seems to me that Apollo's anger bestows a double meaning.
The burial honors due King Laius were never carried out.
The succession left open... the throne laid bare.
You should not have neglected those funereal rites.

CREON
We were afraid.

OEDIPUS
Of what?

CREON
The great Sphinx.
It kept us from leaving the city to attend to Laius' burial.

OEDIPUS
When I defeated the Sphinx, you as Regent
    offered me the crown.
Now together we shall atone for the crime
    as Apollo has commanded.

[*They kneel.*]

Hear us, you gods who look upon this royal house.
May he who slew Laius find no rest, no home.
Let every friendly hand reject his own.
I invoke Apollo himself to witness what I will say.

Let this man shed his own father's blood as he did King Laius'.
He shall find no pardon from me.
I swear by the throne we both have shared
    that I will act as the son he never had
        and avenge his death as if he were my own father.
And furthermore—
I pronounce the same curse on myself
    should the murderer turn out to be a guest
        within our royal palace.
[*To* CREON.]
Now tell me,
    how was the murder committed?

In battle,
 or as I have heard, by treacherous assassination?

CREON

While Laius was traveling to the groves of the Castalian shrine,
 he rode along a heavily wooded path,
  and briefly stopped at some crossroad
   to let the rest of his retinue catch up.
For he always set a fast pace when he had a mind to travel.
It was during that brief respite,
 unguarded—except for his rider—marauders hiding
  in the brush nearby,
  seized the opportunity,
   and sprang upon our noble king
    to rob and kill him.
They left no living witnesses.

[He turns toward the archway.]

Listen!... Blind Tiresias approaches.
His daughter Manto guides him to us.
He was present at Delphi when I arrived,
 and may shed more light on this perplexing matter.

[Enter blind TIRESIAS led by his daughter,
MANTO. He uses a staff, and wears a
white linen toga draped over his head. He
is in sandals. She wears a linen tunic and
the Roman girdle. Her hair is long, and
adorned with a garland. She wears nothing
on her feet.]

OEDIPUS

I greet you Tiresias, prophet of the gods.
Do you know whose punishment Apollo demands?
For I have vowed to banish this killer from our lands.

TIRESIAS

Most majestic king,
 you must not think it strange of me
  if I've been slow of tongue, or asked for some delay.
The truth is, my daughter Manto only now has come
 from a second ritual sacrifice,
  which after Apollo's recent oracle,
   I ordered to further clarify this new
    and ominous revelation.

She has not reported to me what she has seen.
I thought it best to come directly to the palace,
    so that you can hear for yourself the indications we received.

OEDIPUS

I am pleased, Tiresias.
Invoke the gods, and have your daughter describe the sacrifice.

TIRESIAS

Oh, gods that rule on high.
We humbly ask you once again to speak to us.
Show us the way to obliterate this unholy blight.
Give me the power to see and interpret, through my daughter,
    the godly signs that point to everlasting justice.
You may begin, child.

MANTO

We sacrificed, as is the custom,
    a pure-white bull and a heifer not bred nor yoked.

TIRESIAS

Describe all that happened. Leave nothing out.

MANTO

The specimens before the holy altar were perfect.

TIRESIAS

Did you first arouse the gods with oriental incense as required?

MANTO

Yes, father. I poured the perfumed libation on the sacred fire
    as you so often taught me.

TIRESIAS

How was the flame? Did it consume its aromatic offering?

MANTO

It flared up quickly, and as quickly died,
    only to be reborn again.

TIRESIAS

The picture is not clear.
Did the flame burn clean and rise up straight?
Or did it curl and smoke,
    and hover round the sacrificial stone?

MANTO

Its form changed.
First,
    there were many colors like a rainbow cross the sky—
        blue and gold and red.
Then,
    when it seemed about to die and turn to blackness,
        it flamed anew.
This time, dividing itself into separate warring flames
    that seemed to wrap around each other like fighting snakes.

We poured some wine to pacify the flames,
    but as we did, it changed to blood,
And as it spilled upon the altar,
    such thick, black smoke surged forth,
    I thought we all would smother.
Choking, our eyes burning,
        we backed away to stay alive.

TIRESIAS

Something here shames the gods.

OEDIPUS

So it would seem.

TIRESIAS

Did you quickly prepare the animals to appease Apollo's wrath?

MANTO

Yes, father.

TIRESIAS

Did you put salt meal on their necks?

MANTO

We obeyed your every instruction.

TIRESIAS

How did the animals fall? Each at the first stroke?

MANTO

The heifer went down at the first cut.
The bull, with the back of its neck severed, raised its head.
Then it staggered round in terror till exhausted,
    and toppled over.

CREON
[*Aside to* OEDIPUS.]
I don't like it.

OEDIPUS
We'll let the scene play itself out.
[*To* TIRESIAS.]
Go on.

TIRESIAS
Did the blood gush or ooze from the wounds?

MANTO
The heifer's blood ran full and free from her breast.
The bull's wounds turned inward and did not bleed.
Instead, blackened blood flowed from its eyes and mouth.

TIRESIAS
Did you lift the viscera out?

MANTO
Yes, father.

CREON
[*Aside to* OEDIPUS.]
I hate these primitive rituals.
One would think we are barbarians
    the way we carry on about our gods.

OEDIPUS
There is some merit to what you say.
However, once started there is no turning back.
We'll hear the girl.
[*To* MANTO.]
Continue.

MANTO
The entrails shook in my hand,
    and quivered when I laid them aside
        to examine each of the animal's organs.
The liver was putrid with black gall.
The lungs and heart, both shriveled,
    had been reversed from their natural positions.
How this animal lived is beyond our knowledge.
It was an awful omen.

OEDIPUS
Must we suffer the evisceration of every organ
    before the truth will out?
Get on with it.
My patience runs thin.

TIRESIAS
Quickly, my child.

MANTO
But the worst was yet to come.
For in this virgin heifer's womb was a living fetus.
In front of us,
    it broke its bloody bag, got to its feet,
    attacked the priests with its horns until,
    like its mother,
        was silenced with the sacrificial knife.

OEDIPUS
All right!
I've heard enough!
Now I want the meaning of these prophetic signs.

TIRESIAS
Great evil is here.
There may come a time when you will regret
    having asked for an interpretation.

OEDIPUS
No more riddles, Tiresias.
I want to know who killed Laius.

TIRESIAS
Neither the birds who soar on high,
    nor the rotting entrails of those ill-fated animals
        can reveal that name.
There is only one way to unearth the final answer:
The king himself must be summoned from his final resting place.
We must pray to Hades to unlock his murky realm,
    and let King Laius pass up through Erebus
        to appear once again before the light of day
        to name his slayer.
You must select a man, Oedipus, to assist this evocation.
Our law forbids a king to look upon the dead.

OEDIPUS

Creon,

> next in line to my royal throne,
> you will accompany Tiresias,
>> and execute this rite of necromancy.

If it is Laius who seeks revenge,

> then he will have it.

Now leave me. All of you!

> [*Exeunt* CREON *and* TIRESIAS *together
> with* MANTO *stage right. Exit* OEDIPUS
> *stage left. Once the stage is empty,* CHORUS
> *leaves his seat, dons his mask, walks to the
> stage and again addresses the audience.*]

CHORUS

Of all the fortuitous ornaments that surround us—

> our children,
>> positions of honor,
>>> wealth,
>>>> a noble name,
>>>>> a beautiful wife,
>>>>>> a multitude of friends—

Each is dependent on the uncertain and capricious

> whims of Chance and Fate.

We and our beloved possessions are no more

> than borrowed furniture.

Nothing has been given to us in perpetuity.

Our stage has been furnished with rented properties

> to be promptly returned when suddenly recalled.

And when we hand these playthings back,

> it should be done with grace and no complaint.

For no one has a guarantee of immortality—or even longevity.

Whatever gifts of Fortune we may relish,

> we enjoy them by permission of the god
> from whom they came.

Let us then embrace the gaiety of our children,

> and the company of our friends while we can,

And in return…

> give them the pleasure of our society.

Drain every source of happiness while it lasts… without delay.

This night is not to be depended upon.

No! That is too great an assumption.
This hour is not to be depended upon.
This fragile life must someday end.

Take heed!
We are pursued by those no longer living,
                        entreating us to join them.

[*He removes his mask, and returns to his seat in the audience.*]

ACT THREE

※   ※   ※

It is evening. Enter OEDIPUS, *who walks
to the fresco and studies it. Enter* CREON.
He waits silently until OEDIPUS *turns to
greet him.*

OEDIPUS
Why have you kept me waiting?

CREON
I have only now returned from the invocation.

OEDIPUS
Your face reflects disaster. What is it?

CREON
I don't want to cause you pain, Oedipus.

OEDIPUS
Would you rather wreck the state instead?

CREON
No.

OEDIPUS
Then why your hesitation? Who are you shielding?

CREON
You'll soon wish you hadn't asked.

OEDIPUS
Evil cannot be destroyed by ignorance.
I proved that with the Sphinx.

CREON
Knowledge, like the cure, may be worse than the disease.

OEDIPUS
You'll follow your late king back to the underworld
    in your own blood
        if you don't tell me what the rites revealed.

CREON
What's happened to the right of silence in our free state?

OEDIPUS
There are times when silence can be more dangerous
    than open speech.

CREON
You play with words.
If silence is forbidden then freedom does not exist.

OEDIPUS
If subjects do not willingly yield to authority,
    then authority and the safety of the people
        are threatened by anarchy.
Truthful speech has never been punished.

CREON
I will yield,
    but prepare yourself, Oedipus.

[*Pause*]

Outside the city there is a dark ilex grove.
In the center overshadowing the entire wood
    stands a mammoth cypress tree.
Next to it lie two ancient oaks gnarled and crumbled
    with the scars of age.
The blackberry laurel grows there.
Through this undergrowth flows a freezing stream
    untouched by the surrounding plague.
Here the sun never shines.
Adjacent to this flowing stream is a stinking slime pit
    slowly oozing its putrid contents
        into a muddy swamp not far away.
It is to this secluded spot that Tiresias, Manto,
    and the other priests brought me.
As soon as we arrived the incantations began,
    because here it is always dark.

A pit was dug,
    and burning wood brought from funeral pyres
        was thrown within.
Then Tiresias donned his black funereal robe
    and wreathed his long, white hair with the poisonous yew.

Black oxen and black sheep were driven live into the searing flames.
The screams those animals made still resound in my ears.
With horrific tones he called upon the spirits of the dead
    while pouring blood on the fire
        as it consumed the burning beasts.
Then wine and milk he added to these libations.

His sightless eyes fixed steadily on the ground,
    once more he called upon the earth
        to vomit up its buried dead.
A tremor shook the ground beneath our feet.

Trees began to bow,
    trunks suddenly split apart,
        and the whole forest seemed to quake.
"They hear me," the old man shouted.
And with that,
    the ground cracked open beneath the funeral pyre,
    and those charred, sacrificial beasts disappeared
        into some bottomless pit,
        some empty sickly void,
            and in their place stood the viper's brood.
A horrible roar rose up from what seemed to be
        the very bowels of Hades
    as if Cerberus, that triple-headed hound of Hell,
        had angered at our intrusion.

I saw Plague, the killer of us all.
Soon the appalling shrieks of Horror and blind Fury filled the air.
There Grief stood, tearing at her hair.
Disease, hardly able to stand at all,
    stumbled forward.
Age,
    bowed under its own small burden,
        looked around for a place to hide from Fear,
        menacing us with its frightful form.
I saw each miserable creature.
The blood stopped still in my veins,
    and like a spike stuck into the earth,
        I could not move.
Even Manto was stunned,
    despite her knowledge of these divinations.
Tiresias had no fear.
His blindness made him brave.
He continued to invoke the insubstantial shapes of those departed.

And they came,
    shivering and crowding in the shelter of our grove.
First to emerge was mighty Zethus with Amphion,
    his despised twin.
Amphion was clutching the very lyre whose music charmed
    the stones of Thebes.
Behind him was his wife Niobe turned to stone,
    but somehow moving, trying vainly to gather up
        her children, dead around her.
Next came mad Agave,
    followed by the rout who tore their king to pieces.
Pentheus was among them too,
    form no longer human, but as arrogant as ever.
One creature tried to remain unseen, but Tiresias pressed on,
    and many times summoned up that hidden specter
        until its face looked up and it was Laius.
It was an awful sight!
Blood… gushing from his limbs,
    his hair matted with filth.
And then, like one deranged, he cursed this house.
This is what he said:

> *"Murderous house of Cadmus, you will never*
> *stop butchering each other until the last of you*
> *is dead. Maternal love is Thebes' great sin. It*
> *is not because the gods are angry that you are*
> *dying. You bring it on yourselves. Your plague*
> *has not been brought by the South Wind's*
> *noxious scourge, but by a king who claims a*
> *throne as recompense for murder. But the worst*
> *crime of all is hers. Her belly swollen with unholy*
> *issue gotten there by incestuous rape! My country*
> *rots because this pretend-king defiles his father's*
> *marriage-bed. Violates the very womb that*
> *gave him birth. Begets from his own mother*
> *his own brothers and sisters. I shall destroy his*
> *house. I shall bring Erinys as bridesmaid to this*
> *incestuous bond, and she will crack her whip*
> *and cleave this royal house of shame. I shall*
> *overturn and crumble it to dust, set the sons*
> *to slaughtering each other until not one of the*
> *blasphemous lineage remains."*

There is more. Perhaps you've heard enough.

OEDIPUS
Finish it.

CREON
He then spoke directly to all of us about the plague.

> *"Citizens of Thebes, drive this king from your*
> *borders. He carries death with him. When he*
> *departs, a pure sweet air will sweep throughout*
> *this land and your streams and woods will recover.*
> *Flowers will bloom, fruit will ripen, rivers will*
> *flow, because Pestilence and Death, his natural*
> *comrades, will follow him. He may, upon hearing*
> *of my curse, try quick to abdicate and run away,*
> *But I will retard his steps so that he will go groping,*
> *stick in hand like an old man. And while you of*
> *Thebes expel him from your land, his father will*
> *take the sky away as well."*

That's all of it.

OEDIPUS
So!
This would-be priest conjures up a ghost who brings false
    charges against me.
Charges that have no basis in fact.
My parents are together and content.
What wrong have I done?
My father Polybus, King of Corinth, is alive and well,
    which proves me innocent of patricide.
My good mother Merope is still his queen;
    and so acquits me of the crime of incest.
Of what then am I guilty?
Laius died before I ever touched this land.
Is the prophet wrong,
    or have the gods misunderstood their mission?
Not likely.

More likely the prophet lies.
This priest has called up a monstrosity,
    and uses it to shield his true intention—
    to steal my scepter and give it to you.

CREON
Why would I covet what's rightfully yours?
Why would I wish my sister driven from the throne?
Your accusation of conspiracy is unfounded.
I already enjoy the advantages of royalty
    without its disadvantages.
I have fine clothes, good food.
My home is blessed with many friends
    eager to pay remuneration
    for a favor now and then,
because of my present position.
I live a king's life without any of its responsibilities.
What more could I want?

OEDIPUS
That which you lack. Greed knows no boundaries.

CREON
Am I condemned without a trial?

OEDIPUS
Have I been given a trial?

Has Tiresias heard *my* case?
I am, it seems, already judged guilty.
It was you who set the example. I only follow it.

[*Enter* JOCASTA.]

JOCASTA

Stop it!
You argue like two spoiled children
    vying for their mother's attention.
End this squabbling,
    before it ends you.

CREON

Your husband,
    dear sister,
        has accused me of sedition and deceit.

OEDIPUS

He plots to overthrow me,
    and hides his intention with prophetic threats.

CREON

May I die a damnable death
    if one part of one charge you lay is true.

JOCASTA

Oedipus! Listen to him.
He is our brother,
    and would sooner destroy himself
    than plot your overthrow.

OEDIPUS

What would you have me do? Yield to a traitor?

JOCASTA

Respect Creon's pledge to protect you.
Weigh past reality against present illusion.

OEDIPUS

You realize that what you ask may end my reign.

JOCASTA

I swear on my life that Creon will never turn against you.
Do not dishonor him.

OEDIPUS
All right! I will release him because you have asked me,
    but he goes in hatred.

JOCASTA
[*To* CREON.]

Leave us. I will resolve this misunderstanding.

CREON
The people know my innocence. Only you are blind to it.

OEDIPUS
There is no misunderstanding here.
Go find your treacherous cohort. I wish to question him now.

[*Exit* CREON *stage right. Exeunt*
OEDIPUS *and* JOCASTA *stage left.*
CHORUS *gets up, steps to the stage,*
and addresses the audience. He puts
on the mask.]

CHORUS
There once was a king, Minos was his name,
    who ordered the great inventor Daedalus
        to contrive a vast labyrinth to hold the Minotaur of Crete.
The monster,
    to be fed on human flesh,
        was to have it as its iniquitous den.

But when the great warrior, Theseus, entered the lair
    and killed the voracious beast,
        he managed to escape using Daedalus' famous ball of string.
Minos' two grown daughters,
    infatuated with the Attican hero, left their father
    and sailed away with him.

The king,
    so angered by this act of treachery,
        imprisoned Daedalus and his son Icarus
        in the very maze he made.
Undaunted,
    the great inventor built two pairs of wings
    for both of them to use,
        as flight could set them free.

But before they put them on, the father warned the son
　　to steer a middle course,
　　and keep close to the cooling waters below.
For if he flew too high,
　　the sun would surely melt the wax and glue
　　　　and plunge him into the sea.

Icarus did not heed his father's good advice,
　　but flew instead to match his skill against the birds,
　　and soared too high and near the sun,
　　　　which quickly melted down his wings,
　　　　　　and dropped him into the ocean like a stone.

Encumbered by his broken instruments of flight,
　　he could not free his hands to swim ashore.
Thrashing back and forth until exhausted,
　　he disappeared beneath the briny sea,
　　while Daedalus, hovering in the lower air behind a cloud,
　　　　waited for his son to reappear.
Whenever a man is deaf to reason,
　　he hangs by a thread at the edge of disaster.

[*He returns to his seat in the audience.*
Enter OEDIPUS, *and sits on his throne.*
CREON *enters leading* TIRESIAS.]

OEDIPUS
What's the matter, Tiresias?
Why this despairing mood?

TIRESIAS
Send me home.
That will be the easiest way for both of us.

OEDIPUS
There will be no going home, old man.
Do you think I'm a fool?
I accuse you of treachery and subversion.
Of plotting with Creon to usurp my throne.

TIRESIAS
What has to come will come.

OEDIPUS
Then you admit conspiracy to overthrow me?

TIRESIAS
I admit nothing.

OEDIPUS
I think you do.
I think your actions speak *for* you.
I also believe you helped plan the murder of Laius.
If you weren't blind, I'd say you struck the blow yourself.

TIRESIAS
It is you who are blind.
Is that your kingly accusation?
A sightless man who wants your throne?
Never call upon me again.
And I demand that you carry out your promise to Apollo
    to avenge the death of Laius and banish his murderer.
Because you are that assassin.
You are the unholy defilement in this unhappy land.

OEDIPUS
Who taught you to lie so well?
Did you learn it in your prophet trade?

TIRESIAS
It was you who commanded me to speak.

OEDIPUS
But I did not command you to lie.
You have no power here, nor knowledge of the truth.
You are a fraud!
A blind and witless man.
If you were a true prophet,
    when the Sphinx terrorized the city,
    why didn't you come forward and solve the riddle?
You could have saved Thebes.
No! I came!
I answered the riddle!
I destroyed it!
No one helped me.
And now you try to force me out.
You think you'll stand next to him
                    [*Indicating* CREON.]
    on the throne.
You two will pay for this conspiracy.

CREON

Oedipus,
    step down while you have the chance.
Accept a more humble life.
Save yourself.
Don't wait for it all to come crashing down.

OEDIPUS

Are you advising me to abdicate?

CREON

Yes.

OEDIPUS

I'll see you both dead first. Guard!

CREON

You have a hot mind and are too rash.
You forget your kinship,
    obstinately engrossed in your own self-righteousness.
Deaf to reason and advice,
    you refuse to separate what is true from what is false.
You are like a falling rock,
    that breaks itself apart on the very thing it crushes.

                [*Enter* GUARD *who wears a wool tunic
                with breast armor, and is draped in a
                mantle. His feet show a calf-high buskin.
                He carries a short sword.*]

OEDIPUS

You, blind one. Do you align yourself with his pitiful homilies?

TIRESIAS

Only a fool does not see what others see.

OEDIPUS

This refusal to confess will lead you both to certain death.

CREON

You cannot rule by fear.

OEDIPUS

It is fear that protects the throne.
"Who is feared by many, must fear many."

CREON
When men are ruled by fear,
    that fear will turn against its author.

TIRESIAS
It is not kingly to rule by intimidation.
For even the most despicable of things can be feared
    as are the noxious vermin whose bite is deadly.

OEDIPUS
Get out of my sight!
                [*To the* GUARD.]
Take these two and confine them. The charge is treason!

                [*Exeunt* GUARD, CREON, *and* TIRESIAS
                in one direction. Exit OEDIPUS *in the
                other.* CHORUS *resumes his place on the
                stage. He does not wear his mask.*]

CHORUS
It is well known that rulers who fly into a rage
    to justify acts of retribution,
        diminish their greatness
            instead of enhancing it.
When the young emperor Nero was faced with authorizing
    an execution,
    He said, "Would that I had never learned to write."

What a thought!
Illiteracy stamped at conception
    into the souls of those whose destiny it is to rise to power
        only to kill with impunity in the name of justice.

A king is the soul of the state,
    the people his body.
When the soul rages,
    it is the body that suffers.

But what if the punishment is deserved?
Then mercy consists in remitting that punishment.
I do not speak of wanton killing.
That is savagery,
    and is to be avoided like the plague.
I refer only to authorized murder in the name of the state.

We have all sinned,
    but it is the wise king who finds a way
    to make the crooked straight.
Great is the king who has been wronged,
    and remains unavenged.
For no one is greater than the man who has saved another.

With that said,
    I think I'll walk amongst the statues in the palace garden.
It'll be nice to visit the likeness of old friends.
I'll be back to see this story to its end.
I hope you will, too.

> [*Exit* CHORUS *through the upstage doors,*
> *which remain open. He leaves the mask*
> *on the throne.*]

ENTR'ACTE

ACT FOUR

❂ ❂ ❂

Enter CHORUS *from the garden. He shuts the double-doors, and closes each curtain between the marble columns. He then comes forward to speak to the audience. He picks the mask up, but does not wear it. It is night.*

CHORUS

I must tell you about Gnaeus Piso, a man supposedly free of vice,
    yet of an annoyingly perverse disposition.
One who mistook harshness and cruelty for consistency.

Do you know they have a statue in the garden honoring the dolt?
No matter.
His effigy reminds me of a good story about the man
    worth repeating:

You see,
    this Piso, while commander of a legion in Syria,
    once ordered a soldier to be executed,
    because he had returned from a furlough
        without his comrade,
    as though he must have murdered him
        if he could not show him.
When the soldier asked for time to search for his friend,
    Piso would not grant it.
The condemned man was brought outside the rampart
    and was just offering his neck to the blade,
        when suddenly there appeared his comrade
        who was thought to be slain.
Thereupon,
    the centurion charged with the execution bade the guard
        sheathe his sword,
    and led the condemned man back to his commander
    to restore him the innocence
        that Fortune had so timely delivered.
The condemned man and his friend were led
    into the commander's presence by their fellow soldiers,
        amid the great joy of the whole camp,
    embracing one another and accompanied by a vast crowd.

Piso mounted the tribunal in a fury
    and ordered them both to be executed:
    he who had not murdered and he who had not been slain.
Because one was proved innocent, two would perish.
Piso even added a third member to the execution.
He ordered the centurion who brought the condemned man back,
    also put to death.

Three men were sent to die in the same ignominious manner,
    because one was innocent.
Anger is quite clever at inventing reasons for its madness.

"You!" he said to the condemned soldier,
    "I order to be executed
        because you have been condemned to death."
"You," he turned to the friend, "because you have been the cause
    of your comrade's condemnation."
"And you," he said to the centurion,
    "because when ordered to put a man to death,
        disobeyed your general."

He discovered the means of charging them with three crimes—
    because he was unable to find one.
And they put a statue out there in his honor. Incredible!

Well... let us see
    whether there will be any
        statues for Oedipus
           to be remembered by.

[CHORUS *takes his seat in the audience.*
Enter OEDIPUS *and* JOCASTA.]

OEDIPUS
It seems the gods in heaven allege that I have killed Laius.
Apparently, his own spirit accuses me.
And yet, I know in my heart that I am innocent.
I'm treating it as a conspiracy to have me overthrown.

JOCASTA
And you think it is my own brother who indicts you?

OEDIPUS
Tiresias evoked the spirit of King Laius who made the accusation.
Creon was there to witness it—or so they say.

JOCASTA

So it was Tiresias and his damned black art
    that brought this allegation to our royal bed.
Set your mind at rest, Oedipus.
No man is a prophet, and I will prove it to you.

A prophecy once came to Laius,
    that he would die murdered by his son—
    one born to him from me.
But Laius was killed by a group of renegades
    where three roads meet.
It was not his destiny to be murdered by his son.

As for that son,
    before the milk began to flow from my breasts,
    Laius took the baby from me,
        and left him on a mountainside to die.

He was like a god, Oedipus. Perfect in every way.
The gods' last chance to walk the earth alongside men.
But Laius killed him.
Apollo never caused my son to kill his father.
Just the opposite. The father killed the *son.*
And the Fates have paid him back for that unkindly act.

So much for prophets and prophecies. They are worth nothing.
Disregard what Tiresias and my brother think they saw.
There is no sedition here,
    only two men with overactive imaginations.
If the gods wished to speak to you,
    they would not have used an intermediary.

OEDIPUS

Just now,
    when you spoke,
    a sudden chill went through me.

JOCASTA

A chill? How do you mean?

OEDIPUS

You said that Laius was killed at a place where three roads meet.

JOCASTA

Yes. That is the story we received.

OEDIPUS
I should have made the connection then—
when Creon first recounted it to me.

JOCASTA
What is it that is wrong? What have I've said that so upsets you?

OEDIPUS
I will tell you.
I should have told you long ago,
      but I wanted to cut myself from my past.
Start a new life.
I was ashamed to confide in you.
I thought kings had to be beyond the frailties of other men.
As you know, my father is Polybus, King of Corinth.
My mother, Merope, his queen.
I grew up to a privileged life
      until one day a man at one of our banquets
      had too much to drink,
            and told me I was not the king's true son.

I held my anger in, as was befitting my position,
      and did not challenge his insolence.
The next day I confronted my parents.
My father went into a rage and called what happened
      the ravings of a drunken fool, demanding to know
      who it was that told me this unforgivable lie.
I would not reveal the man's name.
For if I had,
      it would have been the same as killing him myself.

My mother sat silently, looking very grave indeed.
I said no more to either of them, but the incident rankled me.
Soon rumors began to spread,
      so I went directly to the oracle at Delphi
            to discover the truth.
Apollo never spoke to me,
      but the priestesses there said he had revealed to them that I,
      like your own dead son,
            would kill my father.
There is more…
The oracle, they said, also prophesied that I would sleep with
my mother,
      and she would bear children from whom all men
      would avert their eyes.

When I heard the prophecy,
 I knew I had to get away from Corinth.
Without telling my parents, I left the city by night,
 and wandered across the land looking for a place of sanctuary.
One day,
 I came across a place where three roads meet.
Suddenly a chariot appeared.
The lord within commanded that I stand aside and let him pass.
I was young, of noble birth,
 not used to such degrading treatment.
I refused to move.
He was old and arrogant,
 and as I would not back off the road and acquiesce,
  he ordered that his driver run me down.
The driver set the horses on me,
 and had I not in defense put a spear into him,
  making the chariot swerve,
   I would have been trampled to death.
In a rage, the old man grabbed the reins and halted the chariot.
Then screaming,
 he came at me with his sword like some avenging god.
I drew my own and killed him as he rushed me.

JOCASTA

Oedipus. Leave the past alone.
You cannot bring that man and his driver back to life.
You killed in self-defense.
Don't dwell on what can not be changed.

OEDIPUS

How old was Laius when he died?

JOCASTA

He was closer to middle than to old age.

OEDIPUS

Did he have a great entourage with him?

JOCASTA

His retinue was large,
 and the roads are difficult to negotiate,
 but he liked to forge ahead to show his prowess.
I am told that at the crossroads,
 he and his driver were alone.

OEDIPUS
Was the driver also killed?

JOCASTA
Yes, but no one saw the murderer.

OEDIPUS
The number fits, and so does the place.

OEDIPUS
Only the time remains to be confirmed.
How long ago did Laius die?

JOCASTA
It's been ten years since the assassination.

OEDIPUS
The facts all mesh. There's no escaping it.

[*Enter* GUARD.]

GUARD
Sir! Forgive this intrusion on your privacy.
But a messenger from Corinth has arrived
    bearing the official seal of his king.

OEDIPUS
Corinth?

GUARD
He says he is known to you,
    and asks permission to be received.

OEDIPUS
Let him enter.

[*Enter* CORINTHIAN *wearing a wool
toga draped around his waist and head
like a hood. He wears hobnailed sandals.*]

OEDIPUS
Yes, I know this man. He is of the royal house of Corinth.
You may go.

[*Exit* GUARD.]

OEDIPUS
Philias! You old goat!
Did you think I would forget that craggy face?
How did you find me?

CORINTHIAN
The world is not so wide that great Oedipus can hide
    from those who love him.

OEDIPUS
How goes it with my compatriot?

CORINTHIAN
Fine, my lord, fine.

OEDIPUS
Philias, this is my wife and queen, Jocasta.

CORINTHIAN
I am honored.

JOCASTA
We welcome you.

OEDIPUS
Do you still herd the palace sheep?

CORINTHIAN
No, my lord. I have taken up the art of sculpting.
I'm told it's a household raise.
At any rate, it passes time quite nicely.

OEDIPUS
Then you shall one day do my portrait.
But not in stone.
All our marble, its seems,
    is always developing another crack or chip.
It must be bronze.
I want it at least to outlive me.

CORINTHIAN
I'm sure my queen would give me leave
    as this commission would be family.

OEDIPUS
Now, old friend.
What commission brings you from your native land?
Has the plague reached you as well?

CORINTHIAN
We are, so far, untouched.
The news I have is of a different sort,
    though just as difficult to impart.

You have been summoned home to claim the throne.

JOCASTA
What? Is Polybus no longer king?

CORINTHIAN
The king is dead, my lady.

OEDIPUS
See how Fortune toys with me at every turn!
How did my father die?
Was it treachery or disease?

CORINTHIAN
Most peacefully in his sleep.

OEDIPUS
These self-appointed prophets who study Apollo's signs,
    or see the world's end in birds that scream above our heads.
They are useless!
My father lies buried, and no one killed him.
The oracle was false.
His death has left me innocent.
Yet,
    the second part of that prophetic will remains.

JOCASTA
The oracle was wrong. You see that now.
Return home with this old friend,
    and join our two great cities under one strong crown.

OEDIPUS
I cannot.

JOCASTA
[*She takes him aside.*]
Nothing in life is preordained. Life is governed by Chance.
Many men before you
    have dreamt they shared their mother's bed.
It is of no importance.
Let this good Corinthian reunite you in your grief.

OEDIPUS
Dear Jocasta, I can't free myself of this fear I feel inside.

CORINTHIAN
Most noble Oedipus,
    you have nothing to fear from your own people.
Corinth is without a king. It needs you at your mother's side.

OEDIPUS
It is not the populace I fear. It is my own mother.

CORINTHIAN
My king, your mother wishes only for your happiness,
    and anxiously awaits your swift return.

OEDIPUS
I cannot go.

CORINTHIAN
Oedipus,
    I have known you since you were an infant,
        holding fiercely to your mother's hand.
Please…
I must return with some excuse more reasonable
    than maternal dread.
No one would believe me.
Corinth would expel me in disgrace.

OEDIPUS
The Delphic oracle has proclaimed that I will bed my mother.
So you see, we must remain apart.
It is why I left originally.

CORINTHIAN
And that is the reason you banished yourself from Corinth,
    so as not to live incestuously?

OEDIPUS

Yes.

CORINTHIAN

Lord Oedipus, your worries have been unfounded.
The King and Queen of Corinth are not related to you.

OEDIPUS

You are the second man to impugn my birth to my face.
My patience has come to an end.
You will prove what you say.

CORINTHIAN

You were given to them as an infant to raise as their own.

OEDIPUS

Why would they want to rear a child who was not their blood?

CORINTHIAN

Being childless, they felt an heir would give the throne stability
    in a time of great unrest.

OEDIPUS

How does a shepherd have access to royal secrets?

CORINTHIAN

It was I who gave you to them.

OEDIPUS

You? And how did you come to have me?

CORINTHIAN

A herdsman on Mount Cithaeron gave you to me.

OEDIPUS

Why were you on Mount Cithaeron?

CORINTHIAN

At the time I was just a simple shepherd,
    and nomadic, as they say,
    not able to care for you in any proper way.
When I passed through Corinth,
    and brought you to its palace,
    in appreciation,
        I was asked to stay and tend the royal flock.

OEDIPUS

If what you say is true,
  then tell me what no one but my wife and parents know
  about some marks I have upon my body.

CORINTHIAN

The soles of your feet had been pierced with iron
  and pinned together.
It was I who freed you from those shackles.
I suppose the scars remain.

OEDIPUS

A mark of shame I've had since infancy.

CORINTHIAN

Because your feet were swollen they named you 'Oedipus.'
It is why you limp.

OEDIPUS

Who was the herdsman who gave me to you?

CORINTHIAN

I believe he belonged to the House of Laius,
  the mighty king whose throne you now retain.

JOCASTA

Oedipus!
Do not pursue this matter further.

OEDIPUS

Do you know the name of this man?

CORINTHIAN

It was a long time ago.
My memory, like an outworn garment,
  has faded with the time.

JOCASTA

The dead despise the living. They envy what we have.
They want to take our lives away from us.
Do not persist in this investigation.

OEDIPUS

Would you recognize this man if you saw him again?

CORINTHIAN
Perhaps.
Sometimes a familiar face can jog a buried memory.

JOCASTA
If you love me, Oedipus, give up this futile search.

OEDIPUS
It seems my much-lauded birth has been a lifelong lie.
This matter does not concern you.
[*To the* CORINTHIAN.]
Go before my shepherds.
Look for the man you speak of.
If you see him, bring him to me.

CORINTHIAN
I'll go at once.

[*Exit* CORINTHIAN.]

JOCASTA
Oedipus,
    if you value our lives together,
        cease this fruitless pursuit.
It will lead to ruin.
OEDIPUS
I must know who I am!

JOCASTA

He that forces truth, forces it to his own harm.

OEDIPUS

The truth can never harm. I must know from whom I came.

JOCASTA

Then I leave you to find out.

> [*Exit* JOCASTA. OEDIPUS *remains
> briefly, then walks to the upstage center
> doors and pulls them open by their ring-
> handles. He enters the garden and sits in
> the moonlight on a stone bench near a
> fountain that is dry.* CHORUS *steps to
> the stage. He dons the mask.*]

CHORUS

He is out there all alone beneath the stars,
   knowing there is no turning back,
   feeling Destiny's pull,
      unable to resist it any longer.

I think we are all like that to some extent,
   clinging tenaciously to a wrong road taken;
      unwilling to admit we've made an error,
     a miscalculation,
        or a changed direction.

I suppose it's only human.
And yet,
   to submit one's self to Fate can be a great consolation.
To be swept up by its cosmic forces,
   is to be at one with the entire universe.

> [*He removes the mask.*]

I really shouldn't overplay my role with constant interruptions.
It breaks the story's natural flow.
Still, it takes time to find an old man
   you haven't seen in twenty years…
   even if the few sheep alive are close to home,
   because the grass no longer grows outside the palace walls.

> [*Pause*]

Think of me as a link that keeps the story going,
    a short reprise to give the offstage action time to pass.

[*Pause*]

A last thought before the play resumes:

[*Pause*]

It seems to me that the answer to our suffering
    is that there resides in all of us
    a divine spirit that tallies up what is good and what is evil,
    and as we treat it, so will it treat us.
But whatever law is laid upon us that we must live and die,
    is put upon the gods as well:
    one immutable stream bears along men and gods alike.

[CHORUS *leaves the stage and resumes
his seat in the audience. Enter* OEDIPUS
*from the garden and closes its doors. He
studies the statue of Aphrodite. Enter*
GUARD.]

GUARD
My lord, the Corinthian has returned with one of your herdsman.

OEDIPUS
Bring them in.

[*The* GUARD *motions off stage, and
the* CORINTHIAN *enters with an old*
HERDSMAN. *The* GUARD *remains
onstage. The* HERDSMAN *wears a
long, wool tunic. He carries a staff,
and has on hobnailed sandals that lace
up high on the calf.*]

OEDIPUS
[*To the* CORINTHIAN.]
Is this the man you spoke of?

CORINTHIAN
This is the man.

OEDIPUS
You! Come here. Look me in the face.
When Laius was your king were you his herdsman?

HERDSMAN

Aye.

OEDIPUS

Do you know this Corinthian?
Have you ever seen him before on the hills of Cithaeron?

HERDSMAN

Why should I have seen him?

CORINTHIAN

Surely you remember.
We used to run our flocks together on those very slopes.

HERDSMAN

I cannot say for sure.

OEDIPUS

Do you know me?

HERDSMAN

You are the king.

OEDIPUS

Did you know me before I was king?

HERDSMAN

I am uncertain.

OEDIPUS

You have either seen me before I came to Thebes,
    or you have not.
Think carefully, old man.
I play no games with you.

HERDSMAN

My… memory… falters.

OEDIPUS

Did you once give a male child to this Corinthian
    on the bluffs of Cithaeron? Speak!

HERDSMAN

I… I… am… not… sure.

OEDIPUS
Why do your cheeks change color?
Why do you stumble for words?

CORINTHIAN
Sir.
Don't you remember giving me an infant one day
    while we herded together, saying,
        "Take care of it. Raise it as your own,
        for I am too far in middle-years to bear this responsibility."

HERDSMAN
I don't understand what you want from me.

OEDIPUS
I want to know what you did with an abandoned child
    whose feet were pierced and bound together like a slave.

HERDSMAN
How could you know that?

OEDIPUS
Then you do know about this child.

HERDSMAN
I am pledged to secrecy.

OEDIPUS
By whom?

HERDSMAN
By our former king.

OEDIPUS
I am your king now,
    and you will answer to me.
Did you give this man such a child?

HERDSMAN
I cannot break my oath.

OEDIPUS
I will break your back if you do not answer me.

HERDSMAN
May the gods forgive me for what I am about to say.
Yes. It is true.
I gave this man a baby such as you describe.

OEDIPUS
Was it yours? Or did it belong to someone else?

HERDSMAN
It wasn't mine. I was given the child.

OEDIPUS
From which house in Thebes did you receive it?

HERDSMAN
I swore I'd never speak of it.

OEDIPUS
I'll make your vow come true,
    and have your tongue burned out
        unless you tell me what I want to know.

HERDSMAN
It was from the house of Laius.
I was to hang the infant from a tree by its feet.
Leave it there to die on Mount Cithaeron and walk away,
    but I could not do it.
No matter... The poor tot could never have survived.
I thought this good man would give it proper burial.
It deserved at least that much.

OEDIPUS
Why do you say the baby could not have survived?

HERDSMAN
It was a worthless gift.
The iron bolt that pinned its soles together
    had caused the wounds to fester.

HERDSMAN
The child was half dead with raging fever.

OEDIPUS
Who was this orphan?

HERDSMAN

Pity me!

OEDIPUS

Was it slave,
    or from a royal family?

HERDSMAN

Oh, gods!

OEDIPUS

If you won't speak freely,
    we'll see if pain will alter your reluctance.
Bind him.

HERDSMAN

Please… I am old and sick,
    and have little time to atone for what I've done.

CORINTHIAN

You will not be harmed if you tell the truth.
The boy you saved was Oedipus.

HERDSMAN

Oh!… Oh!… I should have died that day.

OEDIPUS

You will have your wish this very day unless you confess the truth.
I am tired of your evasions.

HERDSMAN

And if I speak I might as well be dead.

CORINTHIAN

You must tell us what you know.
Oedipus is just.
He will not hurt you for speaking honestly.

OEDIPUS

Who was this castoff?
Of what mother born?
Take care you answer straight.
I will not ask again.

HERDSMAN

Of your wife born!

OEDIPUS

Oh, gods in heaven! What have I done!

HERDSMAN

It was their own son, but the king wanted it dead,
  because an oracle had said the boy would kill its father.

OEDIPUS

Why? Why didn't you obey him?

HERDSMAN

How can anyone kill a newborn?
Even though it was dying, I could not abandon it to rot,
  exposed like some half-dead animal.
If what this man says is true and you are that boy,
  then no man living is more cursed than you.

OEDIPUS
[*To the* HERDSMAN.]

Untie him! Go!
No harm will come to you.
                    [*To the* GUARD.]
See that he leaves in safety.

[*Exeunt* GUARD *and* HERDSMAN.]

OEDIPUS
[*To the* CORINTHIAN.]
You have your story. Now return to Corinth,
  and tell them there will be no coronation.

OEDIPUS

Don't look at me. Just leave.

CORINTHIAN

May the gods have mercy on you, Oedipus.

[*Exit* CORINTHIAN.]

OEDIPUS

It's all come true... *I AM THE PLAGUE!*

I've been searching for myself!
Laius!…Why don't you strike me dead!
I am the abomination!
Earth!… Spew up your rocks, your dirt, your molten lava,
     and cover up my incestuous shame!
I am not fit for mortal eyes to see.
Citizens of Thebes!… Throw your stones!
Burn my body with your fire brands!
I am the pestilence!… I am the scourge that blights your city!
Damned in birth, damned in marriage,
     damned in the blood I've shed.

Only one thing left...
To do a deed worthy of my wickedness.
I must see my wife and present her with her son.

> [*Exit* OEDIPUS. CHORUS *rises again*
> *and takes the stage. He wears the mask.*]

CHORUS
All of us are chained to our own destinies.
Some are shackled by a lax and golden chain,
     others are restrained by tight links of a baser metal.
But what difference does it really make?
     for the same confinement binds us all to life.
Some are held by the burden of noble birth and great responsibility,
     others are fettered by low birth and the misery of poverty.
Some bend beneath another's sway,
     others crumble under their own.
All life is vassalage of one kind or another.

And so,
     we must look to whatever good there is…
          in this sacred earthly place.

It is the same in life as it is within a play:
It matters not how long the action takes,
     only how good the performance is.
End it when you will,
     but see to it that the closing moment is well-played.

> [CHORUS *returns to his seat.*]

ACT FIVE

⚙   ⚙   ⚙

Enter CHORUS *and* GUARD. *It is dawn.*

GUARD

When Oedipus had at last understood the fate foretold him,
    and could no longer deny his unspeakable bond to our Queen,
        he gave me this proclamation
        releasing you and Tiresias from further incarceration.
I was about to go and carry out his order when suddenly,
    shouting to the very skies above,
    he cried out in a most appalling voice:

"How long, oh gods, shall I delay my punishment? How long?"

Then cold sweat began to issue from his skin
    and foam gathered at his lips.
I thought perhaps it was the epilepsy,
    and stayed to be of some assistance.
His eyes all glazed, he stared at me,
    and pleaded that I run my sword clear through his heart,
    which I could not do.
Again he cried, the sound of it more horrible than the first:

"Where are the stones to crush me? The fires to burn my flesh?
Send Agave to do her work once more."

He stopped a moment, and I thought the fit had left him,
    but he whispered to me in our ancient tongue:

"Dost thou fear Death? Fearest not.
For death alone canst make you free."

Then he unsheathed his sword, and was about to plunge it in
    when he stopped himself and said:

"Will one thrust settle all my debts?
Who will pay those I've sinned against?
What compensation will my mother and children have
    from this inadequate demise?
Repeated death is what I need, or better yet,
    one drawn out.

Think! Use your famous wit.
Find a way to die and not to die,
*   neither fully to join the dead nor live among the living."*

Suddenly he began to weep,
    and it seemed a torrent of tears spilled from his eyes
    before he spoke again.

"Can not these eyes pour forth no more than salty tears?
Then both shall follow their prodigious spill."

With fury in his voice he screamed—

"I cannot face my mother!"

Stabbing with his fingers deep into his eyes,
He hooked them 'round the balls,
    and tore the bloody orbs right out.
Again his fingers gouged the empty sockets,
    the holes where once his eyes had been.
Not content, his rage mounting,
    he turned his sightless, blood-soaked face to the sky
    and shouted once again.

"Gods of vengeance, you've had your day of judgment.
I've paid my debt. Justice has been satisfied. Spare my country."

I gave him cloth to stop the flow of blood
    and tried to ease his pain.
"Leave me now," he said,
"and tend to more important business."

That is when I came to set you and Tiresias free.

CREON
Take me to where you left him.

> [*Exeunt* CREON *and* GUARD. *Enter*
> OEDIPUS *a moment later, blind. He*
> *taps his way with a cane. He wears a*
> *gold mask similar to what* CHORUS
> *has worn, but with black eye sockets.*
> *Blood flows from under the mask.*]

OEDIPUS

All's done.
The debt due my father well repaid,
    with darkness my reward and consolation.
I wonder which of the gods has forgiven me?
Is it the Delian one who shut the accusing light of day,
    and granted me some solace,
        and my rightful face?

[*Enter* JOCASTA.]

JOCASTA

What shall I call you? Son?
Do you question it?

JOCASTA

Does it shame you? Speak!
Why do you turn your sightless face from me?

OEDIPUS

Your voice restores my eyes.
Your presence steals away my retribution.
We must never see each other again,
    forever separated by earth's vast seas and foreign lands.
If there is another world below this one,
    with its own sun, moon, and stars,
        then one of us must go there.

JOCASTA

No human scheme, no prayer can change our destiny.
The end is written at the start.

OEDIPUS

That is true. No man can alter his fate.
It is the unwritten law of equity, decided long ago.
I was a fool to have tried to elude it.

JOCASTA

We cannot blame ourselves for the acts of Fate.

OEDIPUS

No, mother…we must be held accountable,
    and accept responsibility for what we've done
        with whatever dignity and grace we have left.

Not cast it off to a throw of the dice,
    and then claim impunity.
If you love me,
    leave—
        and spare us further agony.

JOCASTA

Leave? For what? To live as you? An outcast shunned by all?
To spend my life in unrelenting torment?
No!
I have shared your guilt,
    and so must share your punishment.
For not even the mighty thunderbolts of the great God himself
    can expiate my incestuous crime.
Only a blade plunged in can open the way
    to expel my sickening soul.
Come!
Have you not a hand to help your mother to the other side,
    as you once helped your father?

No?
Then I must take the blade myself.

[*She takes it from him.*]

Is this the sword that killed King Laius?
No matter. It will do.
Where to strike? My breast? My throat?
No!
You know the awful truth!
Only one place rightly waits the pointed blade.
So let it plunge its way into my rapacious womb!

[JOCASTA *impales herself. As she topples
over the sword is released with a gush of
blood.* CREON *and the* GUARD *rush in
and kneel before her body.*]

CREON

She's dead, Oedipus.

OEDIPUS

We are all dead.
Has the new king come to claim his throne,
    or just to gloat in private?

The gods lied to us, Creon.
They wanted more than my demise.
They wanted Jocasta back with Laius.

CREON

I am not here to mock you, Oedipus,
for the wrongs you've caused yourself and all your family.
You've paid enough.
Nor have I come to justify the acts of gods
whose ways have always been inscrutable to me.

OEDIPUS

I only want one thing from you, Creon,
    to bury her with proper honor.
She was your sister and the Queen of Thebes,
    and though I loved her dearly,
        this responsibility falls to you.

I will leave this city to remain in seclusion
    on the peaks of Cithaeron,
        the very place my parents meant to have me perish.
Whether I will live or die on that forsaken spot,
    is already written out for me,
        and no longer my concern.

As for my children, you are now their legal guardian.
The boys are almost grown and will no doubt shun me.
No matter...
They have the means to make their way in this unhappy life.
But my daughters. My lovely little girls.
They have never left my table.
Take care of them.
Don't abandon them to wander with no husbands in abject poverty.
For who would marry issue sprung from incest.
Protect them; they are your blood as well.

I leave now to brighter skies above all Thebes.
When I am gone, the noxious fumes will lift and dissipate,
    and pure sweet air will once again return to mighty Thebes.
The great miasma finally ends.

Come, my Fates.
Come, Disease and malodorous Plague.
Come, intolerable Grief and biting Pain.

Come, Pestilence and torturous Death.
Lead me from this blighted city,
I could have no finer guides than you.

> [*Exeunt* OEDIPUS *with* CREON *leading*
> *him out of the city. The* GUARD *then lifts*
> *the body of* JOCASTA, *and carries her*
> *offstage.* CHORUS *returns to the stage,*
> *picks up the bloodied dagger, and speaks*
> *to the audience for the last time. He does*
> *not wear the mask.*]

CHORUS

What is there left to say?
It seems as if the gods just toy with us for their amusement,
    the way our children sometimes toy with ants.
We... unable to comprehend their celestial sport...
    must not condemn what we cannot understand.
Instead, it falls to us to live with courage and mercy,
    and humbly face what cannot change.

For someday the secrets of heaven will be revealed to us,
    and all our ignorant darkness
    will be dispelled by glorious light.

Time discovers truth, and when that time comes,
    all that is sordid and cruel will be banished
        by blinding radiance.

> [CHORUS *places the mask and the dagger*
> *on the throne, then walks upstage to the*
> *open double-doors, turns and speaks.*]

Keep that image of salvation before your eyes. Farewell.

> [*Exit* CHORUS *closing the double-doors*
> *behind him. The lights fade as the morning*
> *sun's golden rays pass through the variegated*
> *window, settling on the mask, dagger, and*
> *empty throne.*]

APPENDIX I

◉   ◉   ◉

Senecan Sources for the New Choral Odes

1 Though men die, art lives on.(*Epistle* LXV.8)

2 When the time shall come for the world to end…
   (*Ad marciam,* XXVI.6–7)

3 The plague began with the sheep. (*Oedipus,* 133–200)

4 Of all the fortuitous ornaments that surround us…
   (*Ad marciam, X.1–4)*

5 There once was a king, Mino was his name. (*Oedipus,* 892–910)

6 Would that I had never learned to write. (*De clementia,* II.i.2–3)

7 Then mercy consists in remitting that punishment.
   (*De clementia,* II.iii.1–2)

8 I do not speak of wanton killing. (*De clementia,* II.iv.1–3)

9 Great is the king who has been wronged… (*De clementia,* I.xx.3)

10 I must tell you about Gnaeus Piso. (*De ira,* I.xviii.3–6)

11 To submit one's self to Fate can be a great consolation.
   (*De providentia,* V.8)

12 It seems to me that the answer to our suffering…
   (*Epistle* XLI.1–2)

13 All of us are chained to our own destinies.
   (*De tranquillitate animi,* X.3–4)

14 It is the same in life as it is within a play. (*Epistle* LXXVII.20)

15 For someday the secrets of heaven will be revealed to us.
   (*Epistle* CII.28–29)

APPENDIX II

❂　　❂　　❂

ORIGINAL CHORAL ODES

[Reprinted from *The Tragedies of Seneca* (Chicago, 1907), translated by F. J. Miller. The language has been somewhat modernized.]

FIRST CHORAL ODE [LINES 140–255]

How you have fallen, O glorious stock
Of Cadmus, you and Thebes in one!
How do you see, poor ruined Thebes,
Your lands laid waste and tenantless.
And you, O Theban Bacchus, hear:
That hardy soldiery of yours,
Your comrades to the farthest India,
Who dared invade the Eastern plains,
And plant your banners at the gates of dawn—
Behold, destruction feeds on them.
They saw the blessed Arabes,
Amid spicy groves; and the fleeing steeds
Of the Parthian, deadliest when he flees;
They trod the margin of the ruddy sea,
Where Phoebus his rising beams displays,
And the day reveals; where his nearer fires
Darken the naked Indians.
Yes we, that race invincible,
Beneath the hand of greedy fate
Are falling fast.
The gloomy retinue of death
In march unceasing hurries on;
The grieving line unending hastens
To the place of death. Space fails the throng.
For, though seven gates stand open wide,
Still for the crowding funerals
It is not enough; for everywhere
Is carnage seen, and death treads hard
Upon the heels of death.
The sluggish ewes first felt the blight,
For the wooly flock the rich grass cropped
To its own doom. At the victim's neck

The priest stood still, in act to strike;
But while his hand still poised the blow,
Behold, the bull, with gilded horns,
Fell heavily; whereat his neck,
Beneath the shock of his huge weight,
Was broken and asunder yawned.
No blood the sacred weapon stained,
But from the wound dark gore oozed forth.
The steed a sudden languor feels,
And stumbles in his circling course,
While from his downward-sinking side
His rider falls.
The abandoned flocks lie in the fields;
The bull amid his dying herd
Is pining; and the shepherd fails
His scanty flock, for he himself
Amid his wasting sheep is perishing.
The stag no more fears the ravenous wolf;
No longer the lion's roar is heard;
The shaggy bear has lost her rage,
And the lurking serpent his deadly sting;
For parched and dying now he lies,
With venom dried.
No more do the woods, with leafage crowned,
Spread out their shade in the mountain glens;
No more are fields with verdure clad;
No vines bend low with laden arms;
For the very earth has felt the breath
Of our dire pestilence.
Through the riven bars of Erebus,
With torches lit in Tartara,
The raging band of the Furies troop;
Dark Phlegethon has changed his course,
And forced the waters of the Styx
To mingle with our Theban streams.
Grim Death opens wide his greedy jaws,
And all his baleful wings outspreads.
And he who plies that swollen stream
In his roomy skiff, though his age is fresh
And hardy, scarce can raise his arms,
Overwearied with his constant toil
And the passage of the endless throng.

It is even rumored that the dog
Has burst the chains of Taenara,
And through our fields is wandering.
Now dreadful prodigies appear:
The earth gives out a rumbling sound,
And ghosts go stealing through the groves,
Larger than mortal forms; and twice
The trees of our Cadmean woods
Have trembled sore and shed their snows;
Twice Dirce flowed with streams of blood;
And in the still night we heard
The baying of Amphion's hounds.
Oh, cruel, strange new form of death,
And worse than death! The sluggish limbs
Are with a weary languor seized;
The sickly cheek with fever burns,
And all the head with loathsome sores
Is blotched. Now heated vapors rise
And scorch with fever's flames the brain
Within the body's citadel,
And the throbbing temples swell with blood.
The eyeballs start; the accurséd fire
Devours the limbs; the ears resound,
And from the nostrils dark blood drips
And stains apart the swelling veins.
Now quick convulsions rend and tear
The inmost vitals.
Now to their burning hearts they strain
Cold stones to soothe their agony;
And they, whom laxer care permits,
Since they who should control are dead,
The fountains seek, and feed their thirst
With copious draughts. The smitten throng
All prostrate at the altars lie
And pray for death; and this alone
The gods, compliant, grant to them.
Men seek the sacred shrines, and pray,
Not that the gods may be appeased,
But glutted with their feast of death.

❁   ❁   ❁

Second Choral Ode [lines 514–619]

Bind you now your flowing locks with swaying ivy,
Brandish aloft with your languishing arms the Nysaean thyrsus!
O glorious light of heaven, attend the prayers
Which noble Thebes, your Thebes, O beautiful Bacchus,
With suppliant hands outstretched here offers you.
Turn this way your smiling virgin face,
Dispel the clouds with your starry glance,
The gloomy threats of Erebus,
And ravenous fate.
It becomes you to crown your locks with flowers of the springtime,
To bind your head with Tyrian fillet;
Or with the clinging ivy, gleaming with berries,
Softly to wreathe your brow;
Now your hair to unbind and spread in confusion,
Now in close-drawn knot to collect and confine it;
Just as when you, fearing the wrath of Juno,
Did conceal yourself in the guise of maidens.
Virgin, too, you seemed with golden ringlets,
Binding up your robe with a saffron girdle.
So the softer graces of living please you,
Robes ungirt and flowing in long profusion.
When in your golden car you were drawn by lions,
Clad in flowing garments, the East beheld you,
All the vast expanse of the Indian country,
They who drink the Ganges and cleave the surface
Of snowy Araxes.
Seated on humble beast the old Silenus attends you,
Binding his throbbing brows with a waving garland of ivy;
While the wanton priests lead on the mysterious revels.
And then a troop of Bassarids
With dancing step conducted you,
Now ranging over Pangaeus' foot,
And now on Thracian Pindus' top.
Soon, amid the noble women of Thebes,
A furious Maenad, the comrade of Bacchus,
In garment of fawn-skin, conducted the god.
The Theban women, by Bacchus excited,
With streaming locks and thyrsus uplifted
In high-waving hands, now join in the revels,
And wild in their madness they rend Pentheus
Limb from limb.

Their fury spent, with weary frame,
They look upon their impious deed,
And know it not.
Ino the sea realms hold, the foster-mother of Bacchus;
Round her the daughters of Nereus dance, Leucothoë singing;
Over the mighty deep, though new to its waves, Palaemon,
Brother of Bacchus, rules, a mortal changed to a sea-god.
When in childhood a band of robbers assailing
Bore you away in their flying vessel a captive,
Nereus quickly calmed the billowy ocean;
When lo! to rolling meadows the dark sea changes;
Here stands in vernal green the flourishing plane-tree,
There the groves of laurel dear to Apollo;
While resounds the chatter of birds in the branches.
Now are the oars enwreathed with the living ivy,
While at the masthead hand the clustering grape vines;
There on the prow loud roars a lion of Ida,
At the stern appears a terrible tiger of Ganges.
Filled with terror the pirates leap into the ocean;
Straight in their plunging forms new changes appear;
For first their arms are seen to shrink and fall,
Their bodies' length to shorten; and on their sides
The hands appear as fins; with curving back
They skim the waves, and, lashing their crescent tails,
They dash through the water.
Changed to a school of dolphins now, they follow the vessel.
Soon did the Lydian stream with its precious waters receive you,
Pouring down its golden waves in a billowy current.
Loosed was the vanquished bow and Scythian darts of the savage
Massagetan who mingles blood in his milky goblets.
The realm of Lycurgus, bearer of axes, submitted to Bacchus;
The land of the Dacians untamable felt his dominion,
The wandering tribes of the north by Boreas smitten,
And whom the Maeotis bathes with its frozen waters.
Where the Arcadian star looks down from the zenith,
Even there the power of Bacchus extended;
Conquered too the scattered Gelonian peoples.
From the warlike maidens their arms he wrested;
Down to the earth they fell in desperate conflict,
The hardy bands of Amazonian maidens.
Now, at last, their arrows swift are abandoned,
And Maenads have they become.

Holy Cithaeron too has streamed with slaughter,
Where was spilt the noble blood of Ophion.
Proetus' daughters the forests sought; and Argos,
Juno at last consenting, paid homage to Bacchus.
The island of Naxos, girt by the broad Aegean,
Gave to Bacchus the maid whom Theseus abandoned,
Compensating her loss by a better husband.
Out of the rock there gushed Nyctelian liquor;
Babbling streams at his word clove the grassy meadows;
Deep the earth drank in the nectarean juices;
Streams of snowy milk burst forth from the fountains,
Mingled with Lesbian wine all fragrant with spices.
Now is the bride to her place in the heavens conducted;
Phoebus, with flowing locks, sings a stately anthem;
Love, in honor of both, bears the wedding torches;
Jove lays down the deadly darts of his lightning,
Halting his bolts of flame at the coming of Bacchus.
While the gleaming stars in their boundless pasturage wander,
While the sea shall gird the imprisoned earth with its waters,
While the full-orbed moon shall gather her lost refulgence,
While the morning star shall herald the coming of Phoebus,
While in the north the Bear shall fear the cerulean ocean,
Still shall we worship the shining face of the beautiful Bacchus.

⟡   ⟡   ⟡

THIRD CHORAL ODE [LINES 870–936]

You are not the cause of these our ills;
And not on your account has fate
Attacked the house of Labdacus;
But it is the ancient wrath of heaven
That still pursues our race.
Castalia's grove once lent its shade
To the Tyrian wanderer,
And Dirce gave her cooling waves,
What time the great Agenor's son,
Over all the earth the stolen prey
Of Jove pursuing, worn and spent,
Within these forest knelt down
And adored the heavenly ravisher.
Then by Apollo's bidding led,
A wandering heifer following,
Upon whose neck the dragging plow,

Nor the plodding wagon's curving yoke
Had never rested, he his quest
At last gave over, and his race
From that time forth, the land of Thebes
Strange monsters has engendered: first,
That serpent, sprung from the valley's depths,
Hissing, overtopped the agéd oaks
And lofty pines; and higher still,
Above Chaonia's woods, he reared
His gleaming head, though on the ground
His body lay in many coils.
And next the teeming earth produced
An impious brood of arméd men.
The battle call resounded loud
From the curving horn, and the piercing notes
Of the brazen trumpet shrill were heard.
Their new-created, nimble tongues,
And voices strange, they first employ
In hostile clamor; and the fields,
The plains, their kindred soil, they fill.
This monster brood, consorting well
With that dire seed from which they sprung,
Their life within a day's brief span
Enjoyed; for after Phoebus rose
They had their birth, but before he set
They perished. At the dreadful sight
Great terror seized the wanderer;
And much he feared to face in war
His new-born foes. Until, at length
The savage youth in mutual strife
Fell down, and mother earth
Beheld her sons, but now produced,
Returned again to her embrace.
And Oh, that with their fall might end
All impious strife within the state!
May Thebes, the land of Hercules,
Such fratricidal strife behold
No more!
Why sing Actaeon's fate,
Whose brow the new-sprung antlers crowned
Of the long-lived stag, and whom his hounds,
Though their hapless master still, pursued?
In headlong haste through the mountains and woods,

He flees in fear, and with nimble feet
He scours the glades and rocky passes,
In fear of the wind-tossed feathers hung
Among the trees; but most he shuns
The snares which he himself has set;
Until at last in the still, smooth pool
He sees his horns and his features wild,
The pool where the goddess, too sternly chaste,
Had bathed her virgin limbs.

⚙   ⚙   ⚙

Fourth Choral Ode [lines 1080–1110]

If it were mine to choose my fate
And fashion as I would,
I'd trim my sails to the gentle breeze,
Lest, by the raging blasts overwhelmed,
My spars should broken be.
May soft and gently blowing winds
My dauntless bark lead on'
And ever on the middle course,
Where safely runs the path of life,
May I be traveling.
Fearing the Cretan kin, it's said,
And trusting in strange arts,
Young Icarus essayed the stars,
And strove to conquer birds in flight,
On false wings balancing.
He fell into the raging sea
And his name alone survived.
But, wiser far, old Daedalus
A safer course midst the clouds pursued,
Awaiting his wingéd son.
As the timid bird flees the threatening hawk,
And collects her scattered young;
So the father watched till he saw his son
Plying his hands in the gulfing sea,
Enmeshed in his useless wings.
So does he stand in treacherous ways,
Whoever goes beyond the bounds
Ordained by nature's law.

⚙   ⚙   ⚙

FIFTH CHORAL ODE [LINES 1193–1216]

By fate we're driven; then yield to fate.
No anxious, brooding care can change
The thread of destiny that falls
From that grim spindle of the Fates.
Whatever we mortals suffer here,
Whatever we do, all has its birth
In that deep realm of mystery.
Stern Lachesis her distaff whirls,
Spinning the threads of mortal men,
But with no backward-turning hand.
All things in ordered pathways go;
And on our natal day was fixed
Our day of death. Not God himself
Can change the current of our lives,
Which bears its own compelling force
Within itself. Each life goes on.
In order fixed and absolute,
Unmoved by prayer. Nay fear itself
Has been by many found a bane;
For, while they sought to shun their fate,
They came upon it in their flight.

⬢   ⬢   ⬢

Greek Drama in Translation

Tales from the Greek Drama
H. R. Jolliffe, trans.

In this excellent book Prof. Jolliffe retells with admirable narrative skill ten tales from plays by the giants of Greek tragedy.
— **William McCann**
The State Journal

A compelling introduction to the great plays of ancient Greece, this book includes Jolliffe's powerful renditions of *Medea, Alcestis, Oedipus the King, Iphigenia at Aulis, Oedipus at Colonus, Agamemnon, Antigone, Electra, Hippolytus.*

xi + 311 pp. (1962, Reprint 1998)
Paperback, ISBN 0-86516-013-9

Aeschylus Prometheus Bound
Paul Roche, trans.
Thom Kapheim, illus.

His translations of Aeschylus are the best I have ever read.
— **Edith Hamilton**

128 pp. (1962, Reprint 1998)
Paperback, ISBN 0-86516-238-7

Roman Comedy

Three Plays by Plautus
Paul Roche, trans.

Plautus made comedy what it is today.
— **Paul Roche,** Author

288 pp. (1968, Reprint 1984)
Paperback, ISBN 0-86516-035-X

Latin Laughs: A Production of Plautus' *Poenulus*
J. Starks, Jr., M. Panciera, et al.

Student Edition contains introduction, facing vocabulary, edited text with notes, oral exercises, and glossary
viii + 129 pp. (1997)
Paperback, ISBN 0-86516-323-5

Teacher Edition contains introduction, exercises, translation, director's notes line by line, chapters on Roman comedy and cultural aspects of the play
x + 89 pp. (1997)
Paperback, ISBN 0-86516-347-2

Videotape is a live, Latin performance by graduate students at Chapel Hill.
(1997) ISBN 0-86516-324-3

BOLCHAZY-CARDUCCI Publishers, Inc.
1000 Brown St., Wauconda, IL 60084 USA
Phone: 847/526-4344; *Fax:* 847/526-2867
E-mail: orders@bolchazy.com; *Website:* http://www.bolchazy.com